"This extraordinary fantasist is still an active writer and a sly one, much given to surprise."—*ROBERT SIL-VERBERG*

"Vance is eventually going to be perceived as one of the foundation blocks of the edifice that is science fiction." —*BARRY MALZBERG*

"Vance knows about childhood, grief, love, social structure, idealism and loss . . ."—*JOANNA RUSS*

". . . perhaps the premier stylist in the science fiction genre. No science fiction writer does it with the Roman luxuriousness and razor-edge control of Jack Vance." —*NORMAN SPINRAD*

"One of the most thoroughly entertaining of all modern fantasy and science fiction writers."—*LIN CARTER*

GALACTIC EFFECTUATOR

JACK VANCE

SF

ace books

A Division of Charter Communications Inc.
A GROSSET & DUNLAP COMPANY
51 Madison Avenue
New York, New York 10010

An ACE Book

First Ace printing: November 1981
Published Simultaneously in Canada

2 4 6 8 0 9 7 5 3 1
Manufactured in the United States of America

Part One:
The Dogtown Tourist Agency

CHAPTER 1

Hetzel composed a letter, writing a crisp and angular hand in black ink, with a short-nibbed pen:

Dear Madame X:

Complying with those instructions transmitted to me by messenger, I traced the person known as Casimir Wuldfache to Twisselbane on Tamar in the Nova Celeste Sector, where he arrived Ianiaro 23 Caean, of the current year.

At Twisselbane, Vu. Wuldfache secured employment at the Fabrilankus Cafe as a waiter, using the name Carmine Daruble. Evenings he worked at the local Mirrograph when not otherwise occupied as a paid escort for ladies in need of such a service.

About three months ago he departed Tamar in company with a young woman whom I have not been able to identify. At the spaceport I ciculated Vu. Wuldfache's photograph and received information that his destination was the planet Maz, unlikely as this may seem.

I have exhausted your retainer, and will ex-

*ert no further effort until further instruction
reaches me.*

                                        With sincere best wishes,
                Hetzel, Vu.

Hetzel addressed the letter to "Subscriber, Box 434,
Ferraunce" and dropped it into an expedition slot. The
case was now terminated or so he assumed. The tur-
bulence of Madame X's emotions would subside in due
course; Casimir Wuldfache, or whatever his name,
would no doubt exercise his austere blond beauty upon
a succession of other impressionable ladies.

The planet Maz? How could such a place draw a man
like Casimir Wuldfache? Hetzel shook his head in
perplexity, then gave his attention to other matters.

CHAPTER 2

Sir Ivon Hacaway decided to conduct personally the interview with Hetzel; the matter was too important to be entrusted to the discretion of an underling. Nor were the company offices in Ferraunce suitable for the occasion; a thousand underlings observed his every act, and Hetzel was essentially an unknown quantity, no more than a name and a reputation in a field at the questionable brink of respectability. Rather than risk a compromise of his dignity, Sir Ivon elected to manage the business in privacy at Harth Manor.

Hetzel arrived at the appointed hour, and was conducted out upon the terrace. Sir Ivon, who disliked surprises, frowned to see not the furtive ruffian he had expected but a personable dark-haired man of obvious competence and a certain calm elegance that might have done credit to a gentleman. His clothes, neutral and unobtrusive, by some trick of reversal suggested not a neutral personality but flamboyance held under careful control.

Sir Ivon gave a perfunctory nod and gestured toward a chair. "Please be seated. Perhaps you will take a cup of tea?"

"With pleasure."

Sir Ivon touched a button, and briskly addressed himself to business. "As you must know, I am chairman of the board at Palladian Micronics. We manufacture a variety of highly intricate mechanisms: robot brains, automatic translators, psychoeidetic analogues, and the like. These articles require a vast amount of hand labor; automatic assembly is impossible, and our products are generally quite expensive.

"A most curious situation has arisen. We have our competitors, naturally; Subiskon Corporation, Pedro Comayr Associates, Gaean Micronics, are the most important. We all market comparable products at competitive prices, and coexist with no more than the usual skulduggery. We are now being afflicted by unusual skulduggery." Sir Ivon glanced at Hetzel to gauge the effect of his exposition, but Hetzel merely nodded politely. "Continue."

Sir Ivon cleared his throat. "About six months ago a company known as Istagam began to market several high-cost items at prices we can't hope to match. Naturally, my engineers have examined these products, looking for areas where economies have been made, without success. The articles are constructed at least to the standard of our own. Who is Istagam, you ask? Well, we're asking ourselves the same question."

From the house, pushing a teacart, came a portly woman wearing a voluminous gown of pink and black silk. Hetzel rose gallantly to his feet. "The Lady Hacaway, I take it?"

"Oh, no, sir, I'm Reinhold, the housekeeper. Please sit down; I'll lay out the tea."

Hetzel bowed and resumed his seat. Sir Ivon eyed him sidewise, a rather grim smile on his lips. He said, "To you this may seem a footling business: a question of a few million SLU.* Rather more is at stake. If Istagam

---

*SLU, Standard Labor-value Unit, the monetary unit of the Gaean Reach, defined as the value of an hour of unskilled labor under stan-

expands, then we—and by 'we' I mean the members of the legitimate micronics industry—are in serious trouble."

"An urgent affair, no doubt," said Hetzel. "However, I must explain that I undertake no industrial espionage, unless the fee were truly astronomical, and even then—"

Sir Ivon held up his hand. "Hear me out," he said testily. "The situation is extraordinary; otherwise I would simply turn the matter over to one of the large agencies. And I must remark in passing that your fee, while adequate, will be something less than astronomical. Otherwise I would do the work myself."

Hetzel sipped tea. "I'll certainly listen to you without prejudice."

In a measured voice Sir Ivon continued his exposition. "Istagam distributes its products from at least three or four depots—all out to the north of Jack Chandler's Gulf. One of these is a warehouse at an inconsequential little town known as Ultimo, on the planet Glamfyre. I don't suppose that you're acquainted with the place?"

"Not even superficially."

"Well, Glamfyre is a rather bleak place, just about at the edge of the Reach. I communicated with our own district factor and asked him to make a few inquiries." Sir Ivon brought forth a sheet of paper, which he passed across the table to Hetzel. "This is his report."

The letter had been indited at Estance Uno, Glamfyre, a month previously by a certain Urvix Lamboros.

Hetzel read:

Sir Ivon Hacaway
Harth Manor on the Meadows

---

dard conditions. The unit supersedes all other monetary bases, in that it derives from the single invariable commodity of the human universe —toil.

Harth, Delta Rasalhague

Esteemed Sir:

In response to your request I journeyed to Ultimo, where I made local inquiry to this effect. Shipments were received at the Istagam warehouse on these dates, Gaean Standard Time: March 19, May 4, July 6. I thereupon made inquiries at the Ultimo spaceport, which is served by the Krugh Line, the Red Griffin Line, and occasionally the Osiris Line. Proximately before the dates mentioned above the following ships discharged cargo at Ultimo:

March 12	*Paesko*	*(Red Griffin)*
March 17	*Bardixon*	*(Krugh)*
May 3	*Foulias*	*(Krugh)*
July 3	*Cansaspara*	*(Krugh)*

I was unable to determine the previous ports of call of these vessels.

With utmost respect and with hopes for your continued patronage, I am,

Uruix Lamboros, Vu.

Hetzel returned the letter. Sir Ivon said, "I communicated with officials of the Krugh Line and learned that these three ships had taken on cargo at only one port in common." He paused to heighten the drama of his disclosure. "That port was Axistil, on the planet Maz."

Hetzel sat up in his chair. "Maz?"

"You seem startled," said Sir Ivon.

"Hardly startled," said Hetzel. " 'Surprised' or 'perplexed' would be a better word. Who on Maz manufactures micronic components?"

Sir Ivon sat back in his chair. "Exactly. Who indeed? The Gomaz? Absurd. The Liss? The Olefract? Incredible. We have here a mystery of fascinating implications."

Hetzel agreed. "The case certainly exceeds the ordinary."

Out upon the terrace stepped a tall woman of striking appearance wearing a modish afternoon gown of brown, red, and gold pleats, with a panache of black feathers in a forehead band of black velvet. Her manner was rather imperious, and she quite ignored Hetzel, who had again risen to his feet, as, somewhat more slowly, did Sir Ivon.

"Ivon, I implore you to exert yourself," said the woman. "Something must be done! Felicia has not yet returned from Graythorpe, and you will recall that I gave her most explicit instructions."

"Yes, my dear," said Sir Ivon. "I'll deal with the matter in due course, but at this moment I am occupied with business, as you see." He glanced toward Hetzel, hesitated, then performed a rather grudging introduction. "This is Vv.* Miro Hetzel, an effectuator. He will be conducting certain investigations for the consortium. Vv. Hetzel, I present the Lady Bonvenuta Hacaway."

"I am honored to make your acquaintance," said Hetzel.

"It is a pleasure," said Lady Bonvenuta in a frigid voice. To Sir Ivon she said, "I insist that you have a serious talk with Felicia. There are often questionable people at Graythorpe, as you well know."

"I'll certainly deal with the matter," said Sir Ivon. "In the meantime, you might call Graythorpe and make your feelings known to Felicia."

"I shall do so." Lady Bonvenuta favored Hetzel with

*Vv., an abbreviation for Visfer, originally Viasvar, an Ordinary of the ancient Legion of Truth; now a low-grade honorific used to address a person lacking aristocratic distinction.

an inclination of the head and returned into the manor. Sir Ivon and Hetzel resumed their seats. Sir Ivon continued his exposition. "So, then—the Istagam shipments appear to derive from Maz, which seems most remarkable."

"No question as to this. Exactly, then, what do you want me to do?"

Sir Ivon darted Hetzel a puzzled side glance, as if wondering at his naiveté. "Our first objective is information. Are the Liss or the Olefract attempting a commercial penetration of the Gaean Reach? If so, will they allow a counterflow? If not, who or what is Istagam? How does it contrive such remarkable economies?"

"This appears straightforward."

Sir Ivon folded his hands across his belly and looked off across the vista. "I need hardly point out that Istagam represents a nuisance which ultimately must be abated. Naturally, I don't advocate sabotage or assassination; that goes without saying. Still, your methods are your own, and they have won you an enviable reputation."

Hetzel knit his brows. "You would seem to be saying that I have earned a reputation for murder and destruction, which you envy."

Sir Ivon turned Hetzel a sharp look, and chose to ignore the tactless jocularity. "Another matter, which may or may not be connected with Istagam. At times I keep certain important documents here at Harth for a day or two, or as long as a week, in order to study them at my leisure. About three months ago a portfolio containing valuable marketing information was stolen from the premises. These papers would considerably benefit my competitors; to Istagam they would be invaluable. The theft was accomplished with finesse; no one saw the criminal; he left no traces, and I discovered the loss only when I opened the portfolio. I mention this matter if only to put you on your guard against Istagam. The people involved are evidently unscrupulous."

"I will certainly take your warning to heart," said Hetzel, "assuming that you decide to entrust this dangerous and difficult matter to me."

Sir Ivon raised his eyes toward the sky as if in search of divine proscription against Hetzel's avarice. He reached into his pocket and brought forth a pamphlet, which he handed to Hetzel. "I have here a map of Axistil, published on Maz by the local tourist association. Axistil, as you see, is a very small community. The Plaza and Triskelion are under Triarchic jurisdiction. The Gaean sector is tinted green and includes the Gaean spaceport, the Beyranion Hotel, where you will be staying, and part of the settlement known as Dogtown. Far Dogtown, in Gomaz territory, lies beyond Gaean authority and is a refuge for criminals and riffraff. The Liss sector is indicated by purple shading and includes the Liss spaceport. The Olefract sector is shown in orange stipple." Sir Ivon became earnest and affable. "A fascinating city, so I am told. A place possibly unique in the galaxy: the juncture of three interstellar empires! Fancy that!"

"This well may be," said Hetzel. "Now, as to my fee—"

Sir Ivon held up his hand. "Let me recapitulate. Istagam ships its products through the Gaean spaceport. Where do they originate? There would seem three possibilities. In the Liss Empire, or in the Olefract Empire, or on the planet Maz itself. In the implausible event that the Liss or the Olefract are producing trade goods and attempting to sell them across the Reach, the matter is vastly important. Both Liss and Olefract are xenophobic; they would tolerate no retaliation in kind. So, then—Maz. Implausible again. The Gomaz, for all their remarkable qualities, lack discipline; it is difficult to imagine a group of Gomaz warriors occupied at an assembly line." Sir Ivon spread out his hands. "So there you have it: a fascinating puzzle."

"Quite so. And now, a matter of considerable importance—"

"Your fee." Sir Ivon cleared his throat. "I am authorized to pay what I consider a most generous sum—thirty SLU per diem, plus adequate expenses, and a bonus should your work prove highly satisfactory, that is to say, should our maximum objectives be achieved."

Hetzel sat frozen with wonder. "Surely you are joking!"

"Let us not bore each other with spurious histrionics," said Sir Ivon. Your circumstances are known to me; you are a clever man, with the soul of a nomad and pretensions beyond your class. You are currently living at a rather disreputable inn, which suggests—"

Hetzel said, "You have not achieved eminence through tact or flattery, so much is clear. But your attitude clears the air, in that I can now freely state my opinion of the commercial mentality—"

"My time is too valuable to be spent on impudence or psychoanalysis," said Sir Ivon. "Now then, let us—"

"A moment," said Hetzel. "I am normally too proud to haggle, but I must meet you on your own ground. You put forward a ridiculous figure. I could counter with another as unreal, but I prefer to state my minimum requirements at the beginning."

"Such as what?"

"You have come to me because you know my reputation for subtlety, resource, and competence; you want to derive the beneficial use of these qualities. They do not come cheap. You may write your co...ract to the tune of a hundred SLU per standard Gaean day, plus a cash advance of five thousand SLU for necessary expenses and an open draft upon the bank of Axistil, should additional sums be required, plus a bonus of five thousand SLU should the investigation be completed to your satisfaction within the month, with the clear understanding that 'investigation' does not include murder, theft, destruction, or suicide, unless necessary."

Sir Ivon's face became pink. "I never conceived demands so capricious as these! Certain of your remarks have merit, and I might be willing to adjust my preliminary figure . . ."

The conversation continued an hour before a final understanding was reached; Hetzel agreed to depart at once for Maz, at the edge of the Gaean Reach.

Sir Ivon, once more composed, gave Hetzel final instructions. "The Gaean representative at the Triarchy is Sir Estevan Tristo. I suggest that you immediately introduce yourself and explain your purposes; there is no reason why he should not give you all aid possible."

"In cases such as this," said Hetzel, "the obvious and reasonable courses of action are usually the least productive. However, I must start somewhere; why not with Sir Estevan Tristo?"

CHAPTER 3

Maz, a small world submerged under a heavy atmosphere, swung around the white dwarf sun Khis, in company with a large frigid moon. A nimbus of smoky orange, unique in Hetzel's experience, surrounded Maz, nor had he ever seen a moon so gland, blank, and featureless—a globe of frosted silver.

The passenger packet *Emma Noaker* of the Barbanic Line made the required rendezvous with the Triarchic patrol ships. The Liss and the Olefract vessels drifted above and to the side, and all the passengers craned their necks to study the artifacts of these exotic transgalactic intelligences, who allowed so little to be known of themselves. From the Gaean corvette came a pilot to take the *Emma Noaker* down to Axistil and to ensure against the landing of illicit weapons.

Down dropped the packet. The landscape of Maz was that of an ancient world—a half-dozen shallow seas, a few ranges of low hills separated by swamps or undulating plains, with sluggish rivers meandering here and there like the veins on the back of an old man's hand.

Axistil, headquarters of the Triarchic superintendency, occupied a site on a low plateau somewhat to the north of the equator. Halfway into the morning, local time, the *Emma Noaker* grounded at the Gaean spaceport half a mile east of the Triskelion. Landing formalities were brief; in company with thirty or forty other

Gaeans, mostly tourists, Hetzel was passed into the depot. He immediately telephoned the Beyranion Hotel to confirm his reservation, and learned that he had been assigned their choicest accommodations, a suite in the garden annex, at a rate considerably higher than he would have been content to pay had he been settling his own account. A carryall from the Beyranion was on hand; Hetzel entrusted his valise to the driver and set out on foot along the Last Mile, toward the Plaza of the Triarchy.

A world eerily beautiful, thought Hetzel. To look up at the sky was like looking off into sea-green water. Halfway along its morning arc the white star Khis glittered like a sequin. To the left a wasteland mounded with hummocks of moss faded into haze; to the right, a similar landscape sloped down into that nondescript clutter of shacks, huts and a few substantial buildings of whitewashed marl known as Dogtown. Ahead, the structures of Axistil, blurred by the haze, were perceived only as a set of unlikely silhouettes.

Hetzel met no one along the way; indeed, during his entire stay, the disparity between the monumental structures of Axistil and the near absence of a population produced a unique, almost hallucinatory quality, as if Axistil were no more than a titanic stage setting bereft of players.

The Last Mile ended at the Plaza. Here a sign read:

> *You stand at the edge of the Gaean Reach, and are about to enter Triarchic jurisdiction. Conventional behavior is required and will usually provoke no unforeseen inconveniences. It is most wise, however, to obtain a copy of* Special Regulations *at the Triskelion or at your hotel, and be thereby guided.*
>
> Urgent warning: *never venture into enclaves*

*of the Liss or the Olefract, at the certain risk
of profoundly unpleasant consequences.*

*Attempt no familiarity with the indigenous
Gomaz! At Axistil they are normally not aggressive; however, they react unpredictably to
attempts at social intercourse. You may observe them as closely as you like, but do not
touch them or attempt conversation. The
Gomaz are adept telepaths; the extent, however, to which they can comprehend human
thought is still a matter of conjecture.*

Most important! *Do not offer, present, dis-
ply, barter, or sell weapons to the Gomaz! The
penalty is confinement for life in the Exhibitory. There are no exceptions; the regu-
lation is strictly enforced by the Triarchs, two
of whom are Liss and Olefract. Neither sym-
pathizes with adventurous folly or drunken
bravado. If you violate this rule, your visit to
Maz will surely terminate in tragedy.*

A rather dampening notice, thought Hetzel. The ordinary touristic pleasures all seemed punishable by
death, lifetime imprisonment, or unpredictable attack.
Still, this very thrill of danger no doubt accented the zest
of a visit to Maz.

Hetzel took a step forward and thereby departed the
Gaean Reach. He walked out upon the Plaza, an expanse paved with silver-gray schist that seemed to give
off a glimmering light of its own. To one side loomed the
spires, domes, eccentric columns, and asymmetric
blocks of the Triskelion—a structure designed in three
segments by the architects of three races, a remarkable
unique edifice. Beyond the Triskelion, to southwest and
northwest, lay the Liss and Olefract sectors, each with
its cluster of buildings. At the north side of the Plaza,
opposite the Triskelion, stood a pair of monuments that

the three empires had conjoined to maintain: the Rock of Pain, where the Gomaz chieftains, numb with the weight of disaster, had surrendered to the Triarchy; and the multicelled slab of glass and black copper known as the Exhibitory. Both objects were encompassed within a small park, where a few trees with eggplant-purple foliage grew from a dim green sward. To the northeast rose the facade of the Beyranion Hotel, to which Hetzel now directed his steps.

The Beyranion Hotel and its precincts constituted the smallest independent principality within the Gaean Reach. A garden of three acres surrounded the hotel proper; to one side stood the new garden annex. Hetzel registered at the main desk and was conducted to his suite.

Hetzel discovered his quarters to be more than satisfactory. The sitting room overlooked the garden, a place of odd colors, bizarre shapes and nose-twitching scents. Black spindle trees as tall as the hotel shaded tussocks of purple-black moss; from a pond grew clumps of horsetail with pewter stems and orange whisks. There were banks of blue geraniums, twinkling candle blossom, and Maz mint, all of which added pungency to the smoky-sour reek of the moss. Newly arrived tourists now roamed the garden, marveling at the exotic growths and unfamiliar odors. Hetzel inspected the bedroom and discovered a view across Dogtown, which he would visit later in the day. First to business.

He went to the telephone and put a call through to the office of the Gaean Triarch at the Triskelion. The screen brightened to show the face of a delicately pretty receptionist with blond ringlets and a rose-petal complexion. She spoke in a voice cool and tinkling, like far-off wind chimes. "The office of Sir Estevan Tristo; how can we serve you?"

"My name is Miro Hetzel. I would like a few minutes

with Sir Estevan at the first convenient opportunity, on a matter of considerable importance. Can I see him this afternoon?"

"What is your business, sir?"

"I require information in regard to certain conditions on Maz—"

"You may apply for information to Vvs. Felius at the Triskelion Information Desk, or at the Dogtown Tourist Agency. Sir Estevan concerns himself exclusively with Triarchic business."

"Nonetheless, this is an important matter, and I must request a few minutes of his time."

"Sir Estevan is not in his office at the moment; I doubt if he'll appear until the next session of the Triarchs."

"And when will that be?"

"Five days from now, at half-morning. After the session, he allows an occasional interview. Are you a journalist?"

"Something of the sort. Perhaps I could see him at his home?"

"No, sir." The girl's features, as clear and delicate as those of a child, showed neither warmth nor sympathy for Hetzel's problems. "He conducts all public business at the Triarchic sessions."

"Ah, but this is private business!"

"Sir Estevan makes no private appointments. After the Triarchic session he works in his office for an hour or two; perhaps he will see you then."

Hetzel tapped off the switch in exasperation.

He searched the directory for Sir Estevan's home residence, without success. He telephoned the clerk at the Beyranion reception desk. "How can I get in touch with Sir Estevan Tristo? His secretary gives me no help at all."

"She's not allowed to help anyone. Sir Estevan has had too many problems with tourists and letters of introduction. The only place to catch him is at his office."

"Five days from now."

"If you're lucky. Sir Estevan has been known to use his private entrance when he wants to avoid talking to someone."

"He appears to be a temperamental man."

"Decidedly so."

The time was noon. Hetzel crossed the garden to the Beyranion's wood-paneled dining room, which had been decorated with picturesque Gomaz artifacts: fetishes; cast-iron war helmets, spiked and crested; a stuffed gargoyle of the Shimkish Mountains. The tables and chairs had been carved from native wood; the tablecloths were soft bast, embroidered with typical emblems. Without haste Hetzel lunched on the best the house afforded, then sauntered out upon the Plaza. At the Exhibitory he paused to inspect the prisoners peering forth from their glass cells—gunrunners and weapons smugglers, who would never leave their cells alive. The pallid faces wore identical expression of sullen passivity. Occasionally one or another exerted himself sufficiently to make an obscene gesture or display his naked backside. Hetzel recognized none of his acquaintances or former clients. All were Gaean, which Hetzel considered a significant commentary upon the human character. Men, as individuals, seemed more diverse and enterprising than their Liss or Olefract counter parts. The Gomaz, he reflected, lived by extremes peculiar to themselves.

Hetzel turned away from the Exhibitory. The prisoners—pirates, outcastes, mad gallants—awoke him to no pangs of pity. For the sake of gain they had sought to arm the Gomaz, heedless of the fact that the Gomaz, if furnished even a meager weaponry and the means to transport themselves, would go forth to attack the entire galaxy, including the worlds of the Gaean Reach, as forty-six years before they had demonstrated.

Hetzel continued across the Plaza, an expanse of such grand dimensions that the structures around the periphery loomed in the thick air like shadows. He

walked in solitude, like a boat in the middle of a lonely
ocean. Perhaps a dozen other dark shapes moved here
and there across the silver-gray perspectives, too distant
to be identified. A curious vista, thought Hetzel, strange
as a dream.

The Triskelion solidified as he approached. He altered
his direction in order to circle the structure, in effect
entering areas in which the Liss and the Olefract exerted
at least theoretical control, and certainly a psychological
influence. He passed a Liss on its way to the Triskelion
—a lithe dark creature in a scarlet robe—and a moment
later he saw an Olefract at somewhat greater distance.
Both seemed indifferent to his presence; both affected
him with a curious mixture of fascination and repugnance, for reasons he could not quite define. Returning to the Gaean frontage, Hetzel felt the lifting of a
subtle oppression.

He climbed three steps, passed through a crystal
portal into a lobby centering upon a triangular information desk. The Liss and Olefract sections lacked both
personnel and information seekers. At the Gaean segment two clerks were more than occupied with recently
arrived tourists. A burly round-faced man in a splendid,
if overtight, blue-and-green uniform stood to the side,
inspecting all who entered with benign contempt. Silver
epaulets and silver filigree on the visor of his high-
peaked cap marked him for an official of importance.
He fixed Hetzel with an especially stern gaze, by some
instinct recognizing a person whose business he might or
might not consider legitimate.

Hetzel paid him no heed and went to the information
desk. The chief clerk, a portly black-haired woman with
a large lumpy nose and a nasal accent, pursued her
duties with little grace or patience: "No, sir, the Triarch
can't be seen . . . I don't care what you heard, he definitely does not receive visitors at his home." . . . "No,
sir, we are not agents for organized tours; we are the
staff of the Gaean administration. In Dogtown you'll

find a tourist office. They operate a number of inns in scenic regions, and they offer air cars for rent." . . . "I'm sorry, madam, under no circumstances will you be allowed into the Liss sector. They are absolutely rigid in this regard . . . What will they do? Who knows what happens to the people they take away—put them in zoos, perhaps." . . . "In Dogtown, sir, you can buy souvenirs." . . . "No, sir, not until the next session, in five days. The public is admitted." . . . "You may photograph the Liss and the Olefract segments of the desk, yes, madam."

The second clerk, a tall young man with a pale, earnest face, was less crisp and perhaps less efficient. ". . . recommend a hotel in Dogtown? Well, I don't know. You'd be far more comfortable at the Beyranion. Don't forget, Far Dogtown is beyond *everybody's* jurisdiction. You could get killed there, and nobody would even bury you . . . Yes, Dogtown itself is Gaean. But don't wander past the green fence unless you're an adventurer. . . . Actually, Far Dogtown isn't all that bad if you keep your wits about you and carry no more than two or three SLU. Don't drink there, and be sure not to gamble there." . . . "No, sir, I have no knowledge or schedule of the Gomaz wars. They take place, certainly, and if you want to be chopped into two hundred pieces, go try to find one. That's why the tourist agency won't rent you an air car without a qualified guide. . . . That's correct, you can't just hire an air car and go off by yourself. It's only for your own protection. Don't forget, this is the end of the Reach—right here."

The portly chief clerk spoke to Hetzel. "Yes, sir, what do you wish?"

"Are you Vvs. Felius?"

"I am she."

"I have a rather unusual problem. I must discuss an urgent matter with Sir Estevan, but I am told that he cannot be reached."

Vvs. Felius sniffed. "I can't help you. If Sir Estevan

doesn't want to see people, I can't force him to do so."

"Certainly not. But can you suggest some dignified way I could get his attention for a few minutes?"

"Sir Estevan is a very busy man; at least, he says he is, with his reports and recommendations and all. We see him only during the sessions. The rest of the time he's off somewhere with his lady friend, or his fiancee, whatever she's called." Vvs. Felius used her prominent nose to produce a disapproving sniff. "I'm sure it's his business, of course, but he simply won't be interfered with when he's not in his office."

"In that case, I suppose I'll have to wait. Do you have at hand any informational material, especially in regard to, say, the opportunities for investment capital?"

"No. Nothing of the sort." Vvs. Felius gave an incredulous titter. "Who would want to invest out here, away from everything?"

"Istagam seems to be doing very well."

"Istagam? I don't know who you're talking about."

Hetzel nodded. "What about the Gomaz? Are they willing workers?"

"Hah! Offer them a gun and they'll pay you all they own, but they wouldn't work a minute for you. That's against their pride."

"Odd! At the hotel I saw chairs carved ostensibly by the Gomaz."

"By the Gomaz bantlings. They put their young to toil, instead of letting them kill themselves in play wars. But full-fledged warriors work for hire? Never."

"Interesting," said Hetzel. "And you believe that I must wait five days to see Sir Estevan?"

"I certainly can't suggest any other way."

"One last question. I arranged to meet a certain Casimir Wuldfache here on Maz. Can you tell me if he has arrived?"

"I have no such information at hand. You might ask Captain Baw; he's the commandant." The woman indicated the burly officer in the green-and-blue uniform.

"Thank you." Hetzel approached Captain Baw and put his question, receiving for a reply first an uninterested grunt, then: "Never heard of such a person. They come and they go. There's a hundred down in Far Dogtown I'd like to get my hands on, I'll tell you for certain."

Hetzel expressed his gratitude and departed.

North of the Exhibitory a wide road paved with what Hetzel took to be tamped gravel and crushed shell sloped away from the Plaza and down to Dogtown: the so-called Avenue of Lost Souls. A wind from off the downs blew in Hetzel's face, smelling of smoke and peat and exhalations less familiar. Hetzel was alone on the road, and again felt the brush of dream time. . . .He stopped short and bent to study the road. The bits of shell and gravel of the surface were not, as he had first assumed, tamped or rolled; they quite clearly had been fitted piece by piece into cement, to form a mosaic. Hetzel looked back the way he had come, then down to Dogtown. An enormous amount of toil had been expended on this road.

Two tall spindle trees loomed over the road; Hetzel passed below and into Dogtown. The Avenue of Lost Souls broadened to become a plaza, the center of which had been dedicated to a park where grew thickets of cardinal bush, Cyprian torch, and flowering yellow acacia; under the water-green sky and against the somber downs to the north, the scarlets and lemons and golds made a peculiarly gratifying contrast. The structures surrounding lacked uniformity except for a certain easy shabbiness. Timber, marl, stucco, vitrified soil, slag bricks, all figured in the schemes of construction, which were as various as the men who had chosen to build out here at the brink of the Reach. Shops sold imported foods, hardware, and sundries; there were four or five taverns, as many hotels of greater or lesser respectability, a few business offices: exporters of Gomaz artifacts, an insurance agent, a tonsorial salon, a dealer in energetics and power pods. A relatively imposing structure of glistening pink concrete had been divided into a pair of adjoining offices. The first displayed a sign:

> ### MAZ TOURIST ASSOCIATION
> *Information, Tours, Outback Accommodation*

Or more familiarly, thought Hetzel, the Dogtown Tourist Agency.

The premises next door showed a more subdued façade, and was identified by an inconspicuous plaque reading:

> ### BYRRHIS ENTERPRISES
> *Development and Promotions*

Hetzel looked into the tourist agency, to find a similar or perhaps the same group of tourists he had encountered at the Triskelion. They crowded the counter, talking to a pretty dark-haired girl with melancholy eyes, who answered their questions with a charming mixture of reserve, good humor and courtesy.

Hetzel stepped into the office and waited, listening with half an ear to the conversation.

". . . seven inns," said the girl. "They're all in dramatic locations and very comfortable. At least, so I'm told; I've never been out to them myself."

"We'd like to see the *real* Maz," declared one of the women. "The places tourists don't go. And we'd just love to see one of the wars. We're not bloodthirsty or anything like that, but it must be wonderfully exciting."

The girl smiled. "We couldn't possibly arrange such a spectacle. In the first place, it would be very dangerous. The Gomaz are very proud people. If they saw tourists, they'd halt their war and kill the tourists, and then proceed with the war."

"Hmmf. Well, we're not exactly tourists. We like to think of ourselves as travelers."

"Of course."

A man spoke, "What about these inns? If the Gomaz are that sensitive, it might be dangerous leaving Dogtown."

"Not really," said the girl. "The Gomaz are actually oblivious of Gaeans, unless they commit some kind of nuisance, just as you might ignore birds in a tree."

"Can't we visit the Gomaz castles? Like that one on the wall?"

The girl gave the woman a smiling shake of the head. "It can't be done. But some of our inns are built in ancient Gomaz castles, and they're really quite comfortable."

Hetzel inspected the posters: *Warriors March to Battle on Tusz Tan Steppe; the Flyers of Korasman Castle Soar and Veer; Kish Castle at Sunset; Conclave of the Jerd Nobles.* Then he turned his attention back to the girl, who was no less interesting to look at than the pictures. At first glance Hetzel had thought her slight and frail, but on closer inspection he decided that she could bear up very well under a bit of playful rough-and-tumble. He moved a few steps closer to the desk. The girl turned her head and gave him a flicker of a smile. Charming, thought Hetzel.

". . . all seven inns, if you have the time. We naturally arrange transportation."

"But we can't rent our own air car?"

"Not without one of our guides. It really wouldn't be safe, and it's also against Triarchic regulations."

"Well, we'll think it over. Which is the best tavern in Dogtown—the most typical and picturesque?"

"I think they're pretty much alike. You might try the Last Resort, across the square."

"Thank you." The tourists departed. The girl looked at Hetzel. "Yes, sir?"

Hetzel approached the counter. "I don't quite know

what I want to ask you."

"There must be something."

"The situation is this. A friend of mine has come into some money, and now he wants to invest it. The question is: where?"

The girl laughed incredulously. "You want *my* advice?"

"Certainly. Unconventional ideas are the best, because they haven't occurred to anyone else. Assume that I'm about to place a million SLU in your hands. What would you do with it?"

"I'd buy a ticket out of here," said the girl. "But that isn't what your friend has in mind."

"Let me put the matter this way: how could a person invest here on Maz and hope to make a profit?"

"That's quite a problem. The only people in Dogtown who seem to make money are the tavern keepers."

"I was thinking of enterprises on a larger scale, somewhat on the order of Istagam. In fact, where would I find the director of Istagam? I'd like to have his advice."

The girl gave him a curious side glance that Hetzel could not interpret. She said, "That's something I know nothing about."

"Surely you're aware of Istagam's existence?"

"That, and not much more. But why don't you talk to Vv. Byrrhis? He's far more expert than I am on such subjects." She looked toward a door that connected to the adjoining office. "But I don't think he's in just now."

"What are Vv. Byrrhis' enterprises? Or is he a broker?"

"Vv. Byrrhis has his fingers in almost everything: tourist agency, back-country inns, air-car rental. He also operates Maz Transport for the Triarchy."

"Maz Transport?"

"Just old air buses that bring Gomaz into Axistil and back to their castles. It's a free service; the Gomaz wouldn't use it if they had to pay."

"The Gomaz haven't adapted to a money economy, then."

"They haven't adapted to anything." The girl reached to a shelf and brought forth a pamphlet, which she presented to Hetzel. He glanced at the title: *The Warriors of Maz*. "Thank you," said Hetzel. "When do you expect Vv. Byrrhis in his office?"

"I'm not sure. He comes and goes. You can always telephone."

A new group of tourists entered the office; Hetzel departed. He sauntered around the square, looking in shop windows, then stepped into the Last Resort for a mug of ale. Here he ruminated over his findings to date, which were few and could be expressed very simply:

1. Sir Estevan Tristo went to extraordinary lengths to avoid casual visitors.
2. If Vv. Byrrhis were not directly involved in Istagam, he almost certainly knew everything there was to know about it.
3. The clerk at the tourist agency was not the sort of person one might expect to find in a settlement at the end of the Reach.

Hetzel brought forth the pamphlet the girl had given him: *The Warriors of Maz*. On the cover appeared a sketch labeled: "A Flyer of Castle Korasmus." The Gomaz stood on a parapet, wings of withe and membrane attached to his back. The caption read: "Under favorable conditions the Gomaz flyer can soar in the dense air of Maz. He is able to flap the wings by thrusting his legs and manipulating the forward ribs with his arms. In general, however, the flyer swoops down from the heights to attack his enemy."

The Gomaz, Hetzel learned, were an ancient race, culturally static across a period of perhaps a million years. They showed a generally anthropomorphic configuration, after which similarity to the human race dwindled.

The Gomaz skeleton, partly internal, partly external, was formed of a tough, flexible siliceous cartilage reinforced with fibers of calcium-magnesium-carbophosphate, which on exposure to air hardened into a tough white chitin; this material sheathed their heads and formed the substance of three parallel crests that each sept carved into distinctive patterns of spikes, denticles, and barbs.

As an individual, the Gomaz was typically unpredictable, captious, mercurial, with personal gratification as his primary motivation. Yet in this aspect of himself he merely reflected the character of his sept, to which he was telepathically linked. He was the sept, the sept was himself. While the sept lived, the warrior could not die, hence his absolute fearlessness, and the Gomaz warrior thereby became in human terms a creature of paradox, reconciling as he did total personal autonomy to total identification with a social institution.

The Gomaz wars were of three varieties: wars of hate, which were in the minority; wars of rivalry, economic necessity, or territorial control; wars that no xenologist or sociologist or journalist could resist calling "wars of love." The Gomaz were monosexual and reproduced by implanting zygotes in the bodies of vanquished enemies, apparently to their mutual exaltation, which the victor augmented by eating a nubbin of a gland at the back of the vanquished warrior's neck. This gland yielded the hormone *chir* which stimulated growth in the bantlings and martial zeal in the adult warrior. The thought of *chir* dominated the lives of the Gomaz. The bantlings in their mock battles ingested the *chir* of those they had bested and killed; in the adult battles the warriors performed the same act and were thereby exalted, strengthened, and endowed with a mysterious *mana; chir* conceivably fertilized the zygotes.

The Gomaz used a few glyphs and symbolic objects, but knew neither a written language nor other than the most primitive mathematics, for which telepathic facility was held to blame.

Geison Weirie, the renegade Gaean, had discovered Maz sixty years before, and had recruited a force of Gomaz warriors for use as shock troops against Sercey, his native planet. The Gomaz, quickly grasping the potentialities of Gaean weaponry, subordinated Weirie and his band of cutthroats to their own purpose; they captured a fleet of space ships and set forth to conquer the universe. Their raids took them into the hitherto unknown empires of the Liss and the Olefract; eventually, forces of the three empires, acting in concert, destroyed the Gomaz fleet, captured Geison Weirie, built the Exhibitory to hold him, and placed a permanent injunctive agency of three parts upon Maz to prevent future irruptions. The Gomaz returned to their previous mode of existence, paying the Triarchy the ultimate insult of indifference.

Hetzel glanced through the rest of the pamphlet, which listed the septs, described their peculiarities, and located their home castles on a map of Maz. The Gomaz language, which they used in conjunction with emotional keys or colorations transmitted by telepathy, consisted of whistles, grindings, and squeaks incomprehensible to both the Gaean ear and mind. Communication with the Gomaz was achieved through the use of micronic translators.

Gomaz weapons were few: a three-foot staff attached to a ten-foot bola, to assist in trapping the enemy; tongs worked by motions of the forearm; harpoons of three flexible barbs; a short heavy sword. Elite warriors employed wings to hover and swoop; on the rare occasions when a castle was to be stormed, the Gomaz built siege engines of great ingenuity. For transport they used wagons pulled by domesticated reptiles; their diet consisted of substances gathered or harvested by the bantlings, who performed all the work of the sept.

Hetzel returned the pamphlet to his pocket and called for a second mug of ale. He asked the bartender, "At a guess, how many local people work for Istagam?"

"Istagam? Who's he?"

"The Istagam Manufacturing Company."

"Never heard of it. Ask Byrrhis, across the square; he knows everything."

Hetzel finished the ale and went out into the street. The bartender's advice had much to recommend it, and if Vv. Byrrhis were unavailable, he could always put further inquiries to the dark-haired girl in the tourist office.

Hetzel crossed the square to Byrrhis Enterprises and tried the door, which, somewhat to his surprise, opened. Hetzel stepped inside.

At a desk, speaking into the telephone, sat a stocky man with a square, muscular face and a mane of lank black hair parted in the middle and cut square above the ears, in a style currently fashionable among the planets of the Fayence Stream. Byrrhis' nose was long and straight; his eyes were small and steady; his chin was massive. He wore a loose shirt of embroidered green velvet, breeches of purple-and-yellow-striped whipcord, and a fine scarf of white silk knotted to the side of his neck. The garments were informal, almost festive; the man's expression was agreeable enough; his voice was soft and pleasant as he spoke into the telephone. ". . .very much the same idea . . . Exactly. I've got a visitor; I'll call you back."

Byrrhis rose to his feet and performed a conventionally polite salute.

"What can I do for you?"

Hetzel thought that Byrrhis had terminated his telephone call somewhat abruptly. "Quite honestly, I don't know. I've been asked to inquire as to the possibility of local investment, and it might be that you prefer to keep such information to yourself."

Byrrhis acknowledged the pleasantry with a smile. "Not at all. Quite frankly, there isn't a great deal of scope out here for investment. The tourist business isn't all that big and may not get much bigger. Maz is no longer the novelty it used to be."

"What about import and export? Will the Gomaz buy Gaean goods?"

"What we can sell them, they don't want. What they do want, we're not permitted to bring in. And then, there's the matter of payment. They don't have any means of payment, except a few handicrafts and war helmets. Not much chance for any large-scale operation."

"What of Istagam? It seems to be doing well."

Byrrhis responded with easy facility. "That's an affair I know nothing about. It appears to be some sort of transshipment operation. Maz, of course, levies no taxes, which might mean a great deal to some struggling new business."

"You're probably right. What about minerals?"

"Nothing to speak of. The Gomaz take up some bog iron, but the deposits are pretty well used up. The Gomaz have been working them for a million years, more or less. Maz is essentially a wornout planet."

"What about business with the Liss? Or the Olefract?"

Byrrhis gave a sour chuckle. "Are you joking?"

"Naturally not. Trade is a normal condition, provided that both parties are able to profit."

"The Liss are xenophobic to the point of obsession. The Olefract are incomprehensible. We can deal with the Gomaz easier—far easier. Did you notice the road up to the Plaza? The Kish and the Dyads sent out five thousand bantlings, and the road was finished in three weeks. We paid them in pneumatic wheels for their wagons. But there's no money to be made selling roads on Maz. If I had money to invest, I'd go to Vaire on

Lusbarren and trawl for angelfish. Do you know what
they fetch a pound at Banacre?"

"I know they're expensive. At a guess, two SLU a
pound."

"That's close. And at Vaire, just off the Dal coast,
they swim in shoals."

"It's an idea to bear in mind. I understand that you
operate the air-car-rental service."

"That's correct. It's a miserable business, what with
maintenance and downtime and Triarch directives. A
new one just came through: I can't rent an air car unless
I get prior clearance from the Triarch. Some tourists decided to visit the Disik castle and barely escaped with
their lives."

Hetzel frowned. "I need a clearance from Sir Estevan
Tristo before I can hire an air car?"

"That's correct."

"I'll get one this evening, if you'll direct me to his
house."

"Ha ha! You can't put salt on Sir Estevan's tail quite
so easily. He performs official tasks only at the
Triskelion."

"I'm in no great hurry. One more question: where can
I locate Casimir Wuldfache?"

Byrrhis' face became absolutely impassive. "I am not
acquainted with the gentleman." He looked at his
watch. "Sorry, I've got an appointment."

Hetzel rose to his feet. "Thanks for the information."
He went out into the square. The tourist agency was
dark; the girl had gone home—wherever home might be.
Hetzel returned up the Avenue of Lost Souls. Sunset
was close at hand. Khis showed as an orange spark low
behind the western murk; the Plaza was dim and eerie.
Hetzel found it easy to imagine himself a wraith wandering a dead landscape. . . . He was not wholly satisfied
with the events of the day. He had been forced to ask
questions, and thereby identify himself as a curious
man. If Istagam were illicit, he must have sent tremors

through the organization, and he might well encounter a
reaction. Personal violence could not be excluded. Out
on the Plaza, Hetzel felt isolated and vulnerable; he
quickened his pace. The Exhibitory loomed ahead; the
prisoners could not be distinguished. Two dark figures
stood silently nearby; they watched Hetzel pass but
made no attempt to intercept him? Liss? Olefract?
Gomaz? Gaeans? Their nature could not be distinguished through the gloom.

With nothing better to do, Hetzel loitered over his
dinner. As he was about to leave the dining room, a thin
man in a suit of soft gabardine came quietly into the
room. Hetzel studied him a moment or two, then went
over to his table. "May I join you for a moment?"

"Certainly."

"You are the hotel's security officer?"

The man in gray showed a faint smile. "Is it so obvious? My official title is 'night manager.' My name is
Kerch."

"I am Miro Hetzel."

"Miro Hetzel. . . . Somewhere I have heard the
name."

"Perhaps you'll answer a few questions for me. Discreet questions, of course."

"You might get discreet answers."

"My business concerns itself with an entity—a society, a business, a group—known as Istagam. Have you
heard the name mentioned?"

"No, I believe not. What is the function of this so-
called 'entity'?"

"Apparently it uses the Axistil spaceport to export
complicated and expensive machinery into the Reach.
There's been speculation that Maz might function as a
depot or staging area for goods produced outside the
Reach."

"I know nothing about such an enterprise. The hotel
occupies most of my attention."

"Surprising!" said Hetzel. "The Beyranion appears absolutely placid."

"So it is, at the moment. But consider: a walk of only ten or fifteen minutes separates our clientele from the population of Far Dogtown. Is it unpredictable that the foxes occasionally raid the chickenyard? I recommend that you entrust your valuables to the hotel strongbox— especially if you are out in the annex, our most vulnerable area."

"I will be sure to do so," said Hetzel. "But surely you take precautions?"

"Indeed we do. Our detection devices are carefully maintained, and as often as not, the thief is apprehended."

"And then?"

"There is an investigation. The guilty individual is assigned counsel, who holds a preliminary hearing with the prosecuting official. He is then tried and adjudged. He is allowed to appeal his sentence, and recommendations for leniency are carefully considered, after which an appropriate penalty is imposed."

"This seems a complicated operation for such a small environment."

"Not at all," said Kerch. "I comprise all these functions within myself. I investigate, I prosecute, I judge, I sentence, I execute the sentence and occasionally the criminal. The process often requires no more than five minutes."

"The procedure seems efficient and definite," said Hetzel. "May I order a bottle of wine for our joint consumption?"

"Why not?" said Kerch. "I find myself in congenial company, and there is no better occasion upon which to drink."

CHAPTER 4

In regard to Istagam, Hetzel capitulated the possibilities:

I.   Istagam manufactured its products:
    1. Within the Gaean Reach
    2. Outside the Gaean Reach
    3. Upon the planet Maz.
II. Istagam was an operation:
    1. Illicit
    2. Licit but clandestine
    3. Licit, with the operators indifferent to either secrecy or notoriety.
III. The operators of Istagam:
    1. Would use any means whatever to discourage investigation
    2. Would use misdirection and deceit to discourage investigation
    3. Were indifferent to investigation.

Hetzel considered the permutations of the listed concepts, hoping that some course of action applicable to all might suggest itself, and this in fact was the case. He discovered that he had very little choice but to wait for the next session of the Triarchy, at which he could interview Sir Estevan Tristo.

Meanwhile, supposing propositions I-3, II-1, and

III-1 to be accurate, he could reasonable expect that a certain degree of uneasiness must be affecting the operators of Istagam, and he must conduct himself accordingly.

Hetzel enjoyed three days of leisure. He breakfasted in his sitting room, lunched in the Beyranion garden, took his evening meal in the hotel dining room. He strolled about the Plaza, looked across the frontier into the Liss and Olefract sectors, explored Dogtown, and at all times he attended to the promptings of his subconscious. Once or twice he was tempted to investigate Far Dogtown, but decided that here, if anywhere, the risk might be real.

At the northwest corner of the Plaza was the Maz Transport depot. According to Kerch, anyone might freely ride the carriers, but he might not debark at any of the castle stations. Additionally, the adventurous passenger must be prepared to tolerate the unpleasant odor of the Gomaz. The carriers were slow, the routes indirect, the seats uncomfortable. The pilots of these carriers, thought Hetzel, might well provide meaningful items of information, and on the afternoon before the Triarchic session, he went to the landing plat and waited while the afternoon carrier landed.

Three Gomaz alighted—tall chieftains magnificent in capes of black leather and ropes of braided green feathers. They wore cast-iron war helmets with three rows of spiked crests accentuating their own crests of white bone. Wonderful, terrible creatures, thought Hetzel as he watched them stalk off across the Plaza. They were certainly more desirable as allies than enemies: a concept upon which the Triarchy was based, each party more fearful of conspiracy than of the Gomaz themselves.

The pilot refused even to listen to Hetzel's questions. "Ask at the tourist agency," he said. "They've got all that information. I'm busy and I'm late; excuse me."

Hetzel shrugged and moved away. For want of any better destination, he strolled down the Avenue of Lost Souls into Dogtown. The girl in the tourist office might be leaving at about this time, and if he met her on the street, who knew what might ensue?

The trifle of shiny tinsel which was the dwarf star Khis had dropped behind a field of herringbone cirrus, gray-green on the green sky; the light was rather poor, and Hetzel did not immediately recognize the man who stepped from Byrrhis' office. Hetzel halted, stared, then ran forward. He called out, "Casimir! Casimir Wuldfache!"

The man—Casimir Wuldfache?—hesitated not a step. He turned into the road leading to Far Dogtown, and when Hetzel reached the corner, he was nowhere to be seen.

Hetzel retraced his steps. The tourist agency was dark; the door into the premises of Byrrhis Enterprises was closed, and no one responded to his knock.

Hetzel returned up the Avenue of Lost Souls, and around the edge of the Plaza to the Beyranion.

On the morrow, the Triarchic session, and the meeting, or interview, or confrontation—whatever it might be—with Sir Estevan Tristo.

Hetzel awoke in the dark. What was the time? Midnight? The green moon Oloe, a great gibbous ellipsoid, almost filled the frame of the window. What had awakened him?

Hetzel searched his recollection: a gnawing sound, a faint scratching, somehow sinister. . . . Hetzel listened. Only silence. Now a quiet sigh, almost inaudible. Hetzel lay still a moment, gathering his wits. The air seemed stale, a trifle acrid. Hetzel swung his legs to the floor, stumbled from his bed and out into the sitting room. Here the air also seemed acrid. He ran to the door; it refused to open. To the back window he tottered on legs that felt numb. He threw open the pane, and the wind from off the downs blew into his face. Hetzel gasped, inhaled, exhaled, clearing his lungs. His senses swam; he leaned on the windowsill.

Hetzel awoke to find himself back in bed. Morning sunlight slanted through the window; on a chair nearby sat a nurse. Hetzel rubbed his head, which throbbed and ached. Dreary recollections drifted into his mind. Death gas? Sleep gas? Murder? Robbery? Revenge?

The nurse leaned over him and held a goblet to his mouth. "Can you drink? You'll feel better."

Hetzel drank the potion and indeed felt somewhat better. He focused his eyes on his watch. Today the Triarchy met in executive session. . . . In consternation he saw the time, and thrust himself up into a sitting position. The nurse expostulated. "Please, Vv. Hetzel, you must rest!"

"It's more important that I get to the Triskelion. Where are my clothes?"

The nurse ran to the telephone while Hetzel coerced his stiff limbs into his garments. Kerch appeared. "You seem to be alive."

"Yes, I'm alive. I've got to get over to the Triskelion."

"Easy, then. Do you feel capable?"

"Not altogether. What happened to me?"

"Gas—I don't know what kind. They came into your rooms and set off alarms, but they escaped out the back window. Are you missing any valuables?"

"My money is in the hotel safe, with most of my papers. My wallet is missing, with about a hundred SLU and a few documents. Nothing important."

"You are lucky."

Hetzel bathed his face in cold water, drank another cup of the nurse's potion, drew a few deep breaths. The throbbing in his head had subsided; he felt weak and limp, but capable of ordinary activity. Perhaps robbery had been the motive for last night's incursion, perhaps someone had not wanted him at the Triarchic session.

Too bad for his assailants. They had gained small loot, and he would attend the session. Somewhat late, perhaps, but he would be there. He assured Kerch and the nurse of his viability and set off across the Plaza, trotting, then walking.

The Triskelion loomed above him. Hetzel referred to his watch. If the session began punctually, on the hour, he would be late. He mounted the three wide steps, crossed the forecourt. As he reached to push open the crystal portal, it slid abruptly wide, and Hetzel was thrust aside by the furious passage of a Gomaz warrior. Hetzel received an instant impression of a pinched face of polished bone, black optic balls blazing with an inner star; he sensed the creature's rancid odor; then it was gone in a jangle of chain and medals, striding off across the Plaza. Hetzel looked after it, thinking to recognize one of the Gomaz who alighted from the carrier on the previous evening. Where were its fellows? Odd, thought Hetzel. Why should the creature act in this fashion?

He continued into the central lobby and immediately sensed stress and excitement. At the Gaean leg of the reception desk, portly Vvs. Felius stood quivering and pale; the young man leaned forward peering toward a curved flight of stairs.

Hetzel approached. "I came to attend the session," he told the young man. "I hope I'm not too late."

Vvs. Felius emitted a choking, half-hysterical laugh. "Too late, ha ha! Too late indeed! There'll be no session now! No more sessions ever; they've all been killed!"

The young man muttered, "Come now, Vvs. Felius; control yourself."

"No, Vv. Kylo, let me be; it's all so terrible!"

"What's this?" asked Hetzel. "Who's been killed?"

"The Triarchs—all! Poor Sir Estevan, ah, poor man!"

Vv. Kylo spoke in annoyance, "Just a minute; we don't really know what's happened. There's Captain Baw; he'll tell us the facts."

Vvs. Felius called out, "Captain Baw, oh, Captain

Baw! Whatever in the world has happened?"

Captain Baw, his round face pink and purposeful, his mouth coiled into a rosebud, paused by the desk. "Assassination, that's what's happened."

"Oh, Captain Baw, how dreadful! And who—?"

"The Liss and Olefract Triarchs—both struck down, and a pair of Gomaz as well."

"Ah! Aliens all. But what of Sir Estevan?"

"I called a warning to him; he dropped behind his desk and escaped by the flicker of an eyelash."

"Great praise!" cawed Vvs. Felius, rolling up her eyes. "I vow a thousand pastilles for the Sacred Arch!"

Vv. Kylo said, "Vow the pastilles instead to Captain Baw; he seems to have been the hero of the occasion."

"I did no more than my duty," declared Captain Baw. "I'd do as much ten times a day."

"One fact is yet unclear," said Hetzel. "Who was the assassin?"

Captain Baw turned Hetzel a head-to-toe glance under raised eyebrows. He clearly had forgotten their previous meeting. Noting neither opulent garments nor aristocratic insignia, he began to formulate a curt reply; then, meeting the gray clarity of Hetzel's gaze, he cleared his throat and rendered a rather more respectful response. "The assassin was a crazy young Gaean—a vagabond with a grudge, a sectarian, a cultist. In my affable innocence I took him into the chamber, and now you can imagine my remorse!"

"Why, I spoke to that very man!" cried Vvs. Felius. "To think of it! It gives one an utter qualm! He wore no proper tokens, although he was so disheveled that they would never have been seen. Bold as a baron, he asked for Sir Estevan, and I sent him over to Captain Baw; why, he might have killed all of us!"

"And what of this mad cultist? He is in custody?"

Captain Baw spoke tersely. "He escaped. By now he's safe in Far Dogtown."

Vv. Kylo uttered a rather tactless sound of astonishment. "Escaped? With you right beside him?"

Captain Baw puffed out his cheeks and stared across the chamber. He spoke in a measured voice. "I was not at his very side; I had stepped forward to attract Sir Estevan's attention. After the shots there was confusion, and at first I thought to blame the Gomaz, until I saw that two of his fellows were down. By this time the assassin was halfway to Dogtown, curse his heels. Never fear, we'll winkle him out by one trick or another, or maybe arrange his demise. I assure you, he'll not escape so easily."

"A sad affair," said Hetzel. He spoke to Vvs. Felius. "Inasmuch as my business with Sir Estevan is urgent, I prefer to see him now, rather than wait for another session of the Triarchy."

Vvs. Felius said in a haughty voice, "Sir Estevan is certainly too shaken to conduct business at this moment."

"Why not consult Sir Estevan on this score? I suspect that he has more fortitude than you give him credit for."

With a sniff, Vvs. Felius spoke into a mesh. She listened to the quiet reply, and vindicated, turned back to Hetzel. "Sir Estevan is seeing no one today. I'm sorry."

Hetzel stood on the great Gaean porch, wondering what to do next, and not particularly anxious to do anything. In the aftermath of last night's adventure, his legs were flaccid, his throat felt raw, his head seemed to expand and contract as he breathed. Had he been dosed with sleep gas? Or death gas? It would be interesting to know. The ramifications and possibilities were too large to grasp. Speculation at the moment was futile.

Hetzel descended the steps to the Plaza and moved off in the general direction of the Beyranion. He passed beside the Exhibitory and on sudden thought halted to reexamine the apathetic faces. None bore the semblance of Casimir Wuldfache. No surprise, of course, especially if that man he had glimpsed the previous evening had for a fact been Wuldfache.

Hetzel turned away. On a bench nearby sat an unkempt young man in ragged garments and scuffed ankle boots. Matted blond hair and a half-grown beard blurred his rather prominent and overlarge features, but failed to disguise an expression of rage and hate. Hetzel halted to look the man over and received a lambent blue glare for his pains.

Hetzel asked, "May I share the bench with you?"

"Do as you like."

Hetzel seated himself. The man smelled of sweat and filth. "My name is Miro Hetzel."

The young man returned only a surly grunt. Hetzel inquired, "And your name is . . . ?"

"None of your affair." A few seconds later he blurted, "Who are you? What do you want with me?"

"As I say, I am Miro Hetzel. What do I want with you? Perhaps only a few minutes of idle conversation."

"I do not care to talk to you."

"As you wish. But you should know that a man approximating your description has just committed a serious crime. Unless the actual criminal is captured, you would be wise to prepare yourself for inconvenience."

For a moment it appeared that the man would make no reply. Then, in a rasping voice he asked, "Are you the police? If so, look elsewhere for your criminal."

"I am not connected with the police. May I ask your name?"

"Gidion Dirby."

"Have you just paid a visit to the Triskelion?"

"You might call it that."

"During this visit, did you expunge two of the Triarchs?"

Gidion Dirby spoke in a wondering voice, "Two Triarchs? Which two?"

"The Liss and the Olefract."

Gidion Dirby laughed laughed softly and leaned back upon the bench.

"The news comes as no great shock," Hetzel observed.

"I was supposed to kill the Gaean," said Gidion Dirby. "The plan went wrong. After all that work, after all that effort . . ."

"The more you explain, the less I understand," said Hetzel. "In simple language: why did you disregard this complicated plan and kill the aliens instead of Sir Estevan?"

"What are you saying? I killed no one whatever. Not that I wouldn't like to."

Hetzel said thoughtfully, "The description of the assassin—a man vehement, dirty, and wild—is not too much different from your own."

Gidion Dirby laughed again, a hoarse, hacking sound. "There can't be two of me. Sometimes I doubt if there's even one."

Hetzel hazarded a shot in the dark. "Istagam has dealt unfairly with you."

Gidion Dirby cut short his mirth. "Istagam? Why Istagam?" He seemed concerned and puzzled.

"You don't know?"

"Of course I don't know. I don't know anything."

Hetzel reached a decision. He rose to his feet. "Come along with me. At the Beyranion, Captain Baw can make no demands upon either of us."

Dirby made no move. He blinked across the Plaza, then looked back at Hetzel. "Why?"

"I want to hear your story as a coherent unit, especially in regard to your dealings with Istagam."

Dirby grunted and rose to his feet. "I've got nothing better to do."

They moved off toward the Beyranion.

CHAPTER 5

Upon entering the suite, Hetzel indicated the bathroom. "Clean yourself. Drop your clothes down the chute."

Gidion Dirby grumbled something without conviction and went into the bathroom. Hetzel telephoned for a barber and fresh garments.

In due course Gidion Dirby stood in the center of the room clean, shorn, shaved, and dressed in clean clothes. Only his surly expression remained. Hetzel surveyed him with qualified approval.

"You're a different person. Without risk you could return to the Triskelion and assassinate Vvs. Felius."

Gidion Dirby ignored the rather mordant pleasantry. He inspected himself in a mirror. "I haven't looked at myself like this for . . . I don't know how long. Months, I suppose."

Waiters appeared with a catering cart and laid out a meal. Gidion Dirby ate with an appetite he made no effort to conceal and drank more than half a bottle of green wine.

Hetzel presently asked, "What, in general, are your plans?"

"What good are plans? I have none. The police are looking for me."

"Not too diligently, perhaps."

Gidion Dirby looked up, suddenly alert. "Why do you say that?"

"Isn't it strange that an assassin could kill two Triarchs while Captain Baw looked on, then run away unscathed? I may, of course, be overestimating Captain Baw's competence."

"I'm not an assassin," said Gidion Dirby in a flat voice. "Why did you bring me here?"

"I am interested in Istagam. I want to hear what you can tell me. It's that simple."

"Not all that simple. You are a police official?"

"No."

Dirby's voice became sarcastic. "A philanthropist. An amateur of oddities?"

"I am an effectuator," said Hetzel.

"It makes no difference. I have no secrets." He took a gulp of wine. "Very well, I'll tell you what happened to me. You can believe me or not; it's all the same. My home is Thrope on the planet Cicely. My father owns an estate of one of the northern islands—Huldice, if you happen to know Cicely. It's a quiet place where nothing ever happens except the turn of the crops and the hussade championships, and even our hussade is stately and we denude no sheirls, more's the pity. . . . To be brief, I grew up to wanderlust, and when I left Dagglesby University I took a job with the Blue Arrow Line as supercargo. At Wolden Port, on Arbello, we picked up cargo for Maz—perhaps some of this very wine we drink now."

"Not this wine. This is Medlin Esterhazy, from Saint Wilmin."

Dirby made an impatient gesture. "We discharged our cargo at the spaceport yonder and took aboard a new cargo of crated merchandise. The consignee was Istagam at Twisselbane on Tamar."

"Twisselbane? And there you met Casimir

Wuldfache? Or Carmine Daruble?"

"I met neither. We discharged cargo, and then I went across town to the Pleasure Gardens, where I met a beautiful girl with dark hair and a wonderful soft voice. Her name was Elijano. She had just arrived in town from one of the backlands, or so she told me. I fell in love with her, and one thing led to another, and two days later I woke up with no money and no Elijano. When I managed to get myself to the spaceport, my ship was gone and far away.

"A man came up to me and asked if I wanted to earn some easy money. I asked, 'How much and how easy?' This was my second mistake. My first was at the Pleasure Gardens. The man said his name was Banghart and his game was smuggling. Well, I needed money, and I agreed to the proposition. We loaded an old barrel of a hulk with unmarked crates, and they might have been the same crates we had brought away from Maz, except that they were far heavier. But I knew that Istagam was somehow connected with the affair. Banghart told me nothing.

"We took off on the hulk and presently stood off a planet surrounded by an orange nimbus. Banghart identified the planet as Dys, wherever that is. We discharged our cargo by moonlight, on an island in a swamp."

"Dys has no orange nimbus," said Hetzel.

Gideon Dirby paid him no heed. "Banghart approached the planet with great caution, and I believe he was waiting for a signal, because all of a sudden we dropped like a stone down to the night side. We landed on an island in a swamp and all night long discharged cargo by hand, under a beautiful big full moon, green as a gooseberry."

"Dys has no moon," said Hetzel.

Dirby nodded. "We were here on Maz. When the hold was empty, Banghart told me that I had to stay and guard the cargo, that I was to be sent out on another job. I complained, but in a reasonable voice, because I had nothing to back up my arguments. I said, 'Yes, Mr. Banghart, certainly, Mr. Banghart, I'll really guard this shipment.' The ship left. I was sure I was going to be killed, so I climbed a tree and hid in the branches.

"I began to think. I watched the moon; it was big and round and green and I knew then that I was back on Maz. The crates must certainly contain weapons for the Gomaz. I could see that my chances were poor. If the Gomaz caught me, they'd kill me; if the Triarchy patrol caught me, they'd seal me into the top floor of the Exhibitory.

"The moonlight was too green and dim to see by. I sat in the tree until daylight; then I climbed to the ground. The day was overcast and almost as dim as the night, but I noticed a path leading off across the swamp, with timbers laid across the worst spots.

"Even now I hesitated. Banghart had told me to guard the cargo, and I was deathly afraid of him. I still am. Worse now. But I finally decided to try the path. I walked about two hours. I had a few minor adventures, but no real emergencies, and I finally came to dry land. A stone fence ran along the shore. By this time nothing seemed strange. The path let to a gate, and here a man waited, and this is where the story starts to become insane. I'm not insane, mind you; it's just what happened to me. This man was tall and as handsome as Avatar Gisrod. He wore a white robe, a white turban, a veil of white gauze embroidered with black pearls. He seemed to be expecting me. I said, 'Good morning, sir, can you direct me to civilization?''

"He said, 'Of course. Step over here.' He took me to a tent. 'Just wait inside.'

"I said I'd just as soon wait outside in the open; he just pointed into the tent. I went in, and that's all I remember; Handsome must have had put-out gas waiting for me." Gidion Dirby heaved a sad sigh.

"I came back to life in a large bare room. There were no doors or windows. The floor measured twelve paces in one direction, fourteen and a half in the other. The ceiling was high; I could barely see it. I must have been unconscious for two or three days; my beard had grown; I was weak and thirsty. There was a chair, a table, a couch, all built of rough timber, but I wasn't overly critical. What do you think of the story so far?"

"I haven't thought. I'm just listening. Offhand, there doesn't seem any relationship between its various phases."

Dirby could not restrain a grim smile. "Quite right. Where does it start? When I left Dagglesby University? When I first came to Maz? At the Pleasure Gardens? When I took up with Banghart? Or has this always been my destiny? This is a most important question."

Hetzel said, "Perhaps I lack perceptiveness . . ."

Dirby showed no impatience. "The point is this. . . . But, no, I'll just go on with the story. It's quite absurd, don't you think?"

Hetzel refilled the goblets. "There may be a pattern not yet evident to either of us."

Dirby shrugged, to indicate that he cared nothing one way or the other. "I looked around the room. Light came from two high fixtures. The walls were white plastic. The floor was covered with a gray composition. Across one end of the room was a platform, as high as my waist and four feet wide—a stage, with flush doors at both sides. On the table was a jug. It seemed to hold water, and I drank. The water had an odd flavor, and after a few minutes I was bent over with stomach cramps. I decided that I had been poisoned, and I was ready to die. But I vomited instead, time after time, until I was too weak to vomit anymore. Then I crawled to the couch and went to sleep.

"When I awoke, I felt better. The room looked exactly as before, except that someone had kindly cleaned up the vomit, and on the table beside the jug was a photograph of Handsome. Something nagged at my mind. Was I in the same room? The walls were pale yellow instead of white. I stood up, and I was still hungry and thirsty. On the stage I noticed a tray with bread, cheese, and fruit, and a glass mug full of beer. I looked at it a minute. Maybe it was poisoned, like the water. I decided I didn't care; I'd just as soon be poisoned as starve. I picked up the bread and cheese. It was rubber. The beer was some sort of gel. At the bottom of the mug I found a photograph of a man winking at me—Handsome.

"I made up my mind to be stoic. Someone was watching me—a lunatic, or a sadist, or Handsome, or all three. I'd give him no satisfaction. I turned away and went to sit down in the chair. It gave me an electric shock. With great dignity I went to the cot. It was sopping wet. I sat on the table. A few minutes later I looked back at the stage, and the tray had been moved. Somehow it looked different. I sat for a moment or two, then leisurely got up to investigate. This time the food was real. I brought it back to the table and ate. Without thinking, I was sitting in the chair. As soon as I remembered, I began to expect a shock, but nothing happened. This, incidentally, was how I was fed during my entire stay. Sometimes the food was real, more often not. The intervals were irregular. I never knew when I would be fed." Dirby gave a sad laugh. "When the waiters brought in our meal, I half-expected it to be rubber, and I would not have been surprised."

"It seems that you were the victim of a careful and systematic persecution."

"Call it what you like. The food trick was trivial compared to what else went on; after a while, I hardly thought about it. I was never shocked again, incidentally. I always half expected it. And after that first jug of water, the food never poisoned me again.

"When I finished that first meal, I looked at the back wall, which was blue. I was sure all the walls had been yellow. I began to wonder if I were insane after all. The walls kept changing colors—never when I looked at them: white, yellow, green, blue, occasionally brown or gray. I learned to dislike brown and gray, because they usually—not always—meant that something unpleasant was about to happen."

"A very strange proceeding," mused Hetzel. "Perhaps some sort of experiment?"

"That's what I thought at first. I changed my mind. . . . The first few days, nothing much happened, except the rubber food and the walls changing color. Once, when I lay on the cot it tossed me out; another time, the chair collapsed. Occasionally I'd hear small noises behind my back, noises very near—a footstep, a whisper, a giggle. Then there was Handsome. One day the walls turned gray. When I noticed the stage, I saw that a doorway had opened at the back to show a long hall. At the far end, a man appeared. He wore Old Shalkho costume—tight breeches of white velvet, a pink-and-blue jacket with gold tassels, a ruffled cravat. He was a tall, strong man, very stately in his manner, very handsome. He came to the edge of the stage and looked toward me—not at me, but toward me—with a peculiar expression I can't describe: amused, bored, supercilious. He said, 'You're making yourself quite comfortable. Too comfortable. We'll see to that.'

"I called out, 'Why are you keeping me here? I've done nothing to you!' He paid no attention. He said, 'You must think more intently.' I said, 'I've been thinking about everything there is to think about.'

"Again he paid no attention. 'Perhaps you're lonely, perhaps you'd like some company. Well, why not?' And out on the stage ran a dozen beasts, like weasels, with spiked tails and long fangs and prongs growing from their elbows. They ran at me squealing and hissing. I climbed up on the table and kicked them back when they jumped. Handsome watched from the doorway, with an absolutely quiet expression—not even smiling. Two or three times the weasels almost had me; then they gave up and began to roam the room. When one came close, I jumped on it and crushed it to the floor, and I finally killed them all. Handsome had gone away long ago.

"I piled the dead things in a corner and went to look at the doorway where he had stood. The wall seemed solid, so here was another mystery, although now mysteries were simply ordinary events—a way of life, so to speak. Still, if Handsome wanted me to think, he had his way with me, because I did little else.

"I wondered why they worked such elaborate pranks. Revenge? Except for my sad little smuggling exploit, I had lived a blameless life. An experiment with my sanity? They could have proceeded much more harshly. Mistaken identity? Possibly. Or perhaps I was in the hands of some mad prankster who enjoyed practical jokes. Nothing seemed reasonable."

"And did you see Handsome again?"

"I did indeed, and the back wall turned gray before every time, although sometimes it turned gray and Handsome never appeared. But other things happened, silly, strange things. One day I heard a fanfare, then music, and a troupe of trained birds ran out on the stage. They danced and ran in circles and jumped over each other and marched back and forth; then they all turned somersaults off the stage. The music became a caterwauling, blatting and clanging and thumping; then it stopped. I heard a girl giggling, and then there was silence. The girl sounded like Elijano, even though I knew this to be impossible. Then I thought: impossible? Nothing was impossible.

"About an hour later, the lights went out, and the room was pitch dark. A minute or two passed; then a tremendous green flash filled the room, and a clap of noise. I was startled and almost fell out of the cot. I lay in the dark expecting another flash, but after five minutes the usual lights turned on.

"A jailer began to appear in the room—a creature half-man and half-woman. His right side was masculine; his left side was female. He—I'll call it a 'he'—never spoke, and I never spoke. He'd walk around the room, look here and there, wink and grimace, perform some silly caper, and go. He came about five times; then I never saw him again. But one time I awoke and found three naked girls wearing dominoes, crawling around the room on their hands and knees. When they saw I was awake, they ran out of the room. One of them was Elijano—I think. I'm not sure. About this time my meals began to appear in articles of the most extraordinary shape and size: a tiny bowl with an enormous lopsided spoon; a ten-gallon kettle twisted into a half-spiral, with a bit of cheese at the bottom; tangles of tubes and bulbs in which I was served my drink; a tray half an inch across and three feet long holding three peas. I found these amusing rather than otherwise, though I never had enough to eat.

"The lights went out a second time, and I lay on the couch waiting for another flash of green light, but this time the ceiling billowed with luminous gas. It dissipated, and there was a view out over my old home at Thrope. It changed to other landscapes of the neighborhood, and then others I couldn't recognize. All these pictures were distorted; they all shuddered and quivered and crawled. My own face appeared, then the top of my head. Two hands cut away my scalp with a saw, and there was my brain. Eljiano ran away; the picture changed and became a calm stern face—Handsome. Mind you, this was not a dream. My dreams during this time were havens of normality. . . . The lights went on. I sat up on the couch and yawned and stretched, as if I were accustomed to such visions. I'd now decided that Handsome was deliberately trying to drive me insane. I still think so."

Hetzel made a gesture that might have signified almost anything; Dirby turned on him a resentful scowl. "Other incidents occurred. The sounds behind me—whispers and giggles. About every third day the lights would gradually go dim, and I'd start to wonder why I

couldn't see; was I going blind? Then they'd play music
—a simple tune that would meander through all kinds of
meaningless phrases and never resolve, or go through a
hundred repetitions. And of course, Handsome. He
came twice more to the doorway that opened on the
stage, and once I turned around, and there he stood in
the room with me. He wore a different costume—a suit
of silver scales, a silver morion with cusps across his
cheeks, a nasal protecting his nose, and three silver
spikes at his forehead. He spoke to me. 'Hello, Gidion
Dirby.'

"I said, 'So you know my name.'

" 'Of course I know your name.'

" 'I thought you might be making a mistake.'

" 'I never make mistakes.'

" 'Then why are you keeping me here?'

" 'Because I choose to do so.' He went to the table.
'This must be your breakfast. Are you hungry?' He took
the lid off the pot, and there was the contents of my
commode—or somebody else's commode. When I
looked down, he turned the pot over my head, then left
by the door at the side of the stage.

"I cleaned myself up as well as I could, and went to sit
on the couch. Presently I became drowsy and fell asleep,
and when I woke up, I was in a new and different place
—a bench outside a building of iron and glass, which I
saw to be the Maz space depot. I sat for a few minutes
gathering my wits. Could it be that I was free? No one
paid any attention to me. I checked my pockets and my
pouch: there was nothing but a few coins and a zap gun;
no papers.

"A guard came up to me and asked what I was up to;
I told him I was waiting for a ship. He asked for identification; I said I'd lost my papers. In that case I'd have
to get new papers from the Gaean Triarch. Luckily for
me, so he said, the session was just starting, and he set
me off along the avenue to the Triskelion. I went into
the lobby. A big red-faced official asked what I wanted.

I said I must see the Gaean Triarch on urgent business. He took me into a chamber with three desks. There were three Gomaz ahead of me. The security officer led me to one of the desks and said, "This man claims urgent business with you.' To me he said, "This is Sir Estevan Tristo; state your business.' But I couldn't state anything, because this was Handsome. He looked at me, and I looked at him. Then I just turned and walked away, too confused to even talk. Behind me I heard zaps going off. I looked around. Handsome had dropped behind his desk, and there was a great deal of shouting. I saw that two of the Gomaz were on the floor. The official made a dive for me, but I knocked him down and ran out the side door. I had nowhere to go, so I ran across the Plaza and sat down on the bench, and there you found me. I see now that I was wrong running away; I should have stayed and told the truth. Mind search would have proved me out. . . . Of course, they might have shot me first and asked questions later. Maybe I acted correctly."

"Not really," said Hetzel. "You should have continued down to Dogtown. Far Dogtown, that is. Sitting in the Plaza, you're fair game for Captain Baw. Even a confused pseudo-lunatic should know better than to pose invitingly before the Exhibitory. Why did you stop there?"

Dirby's face became dark and sullen. "I don't know. I saw a bench, and I sat down. Must I explain everything?"

Hetzel ignored the question. "You suffered a perplexing experience. At least, from your point of view. Sir Estevan is definitely Handsome?"

"I'd know his face among ten thousand."

"And he recognized you?"

"He said nothing. His face showed nothing. But he must have recognized me."

CHAPTER 6

Hetzel went to the window and stood looking out over the Plaza. Dirby slumped back in his chair and stared morosely down into the goblet.

Hetzel turned back to Dirby. "You are still carrying the zap gun?"

Dirby brought it forth; Hetzel examined the charge meter, slid out the power cell, examined the meter once more. "It shows a charge, but the cell is dead. The meter has been jammed." He tossed the gun aside. "I assume that you were meant to be captured. Some element of the plan went wrong. You escaped. Or were allowed to escape."

Dirby frowned. "So . . . what do I do now?"

"Send a message to your father. Ask him to send out legal aid and a Gaean marshal as quickly as possible. Then, don't stir from the premises of the Beyranion, or you'll be subject to the jurisdiction of the Triskelion. If you were put on trial now, your chances would be poor."

"Mind search would prove that I'm telling the truth," Dirby muttered.

"Mind search would prove that you subscribe to a maniac's dream in which Sir Estevan Tristo is your persecutor. You would be declared criminally insane and guilty of murder."

Dirby growled. "Either way, I lose."

"You don't have a chance unless you can corroborate your story."

"Very well. You're an effectuator. Effect an investigation."

Hetzel reflected a moment. "I have other commitments. There might be a conflict of interest. Still, on the other hand, I might be able to sell the same work twice, which is all to the good. I presume you intend to pay me?"

Dirby looked up with a rather unpleasant sneer. "With what? I don't have a zink.* If you're worried, I'll make out a draft upon my father's bank, which he will certainly honor."

"We'll discuss this in due course. But first an understanding. I commit myself only to investigation. I undertake neither to assert your innocence nor to defend your guilt. You must secure legal representation elsewhere. Is this agreeable?"

Dirby gave an indifferent shrug. "Whatever you say. I'm in no position to argue."

"By any chance are you acquainted with a certain Casimir Wuldfache? No? What about Carmine Daruble? I'd like you to examine a photograph . . ." Hetzel stopped short. His wallet, with eighty-five SLU and the photograph of Casimir Wuldfache, had been stolen from him. "Well, no matter."

A chime sounded. Hetzel went to the door and slid it open, to reveal two men—the first a ponderous and immaculate gentleman whom Hetzel recognized for the hotel manager, and Kerch, the hotel security officer.

"I am Aeolus Shult, manager of the Beyranion," said

---

*Zink, a coin representative of a man-minute, the hundredth part of an SLU. Gaean time is based upon the standard day of Earth, subdivided into twenty-four hours, after ancient tradition. A minute is the hundredth part of an hour, a second is the hundredth part of a minute.

the large man in a dry, precise voice. "This is Nello Kerch, our security officer. May we come in?"

Hetzel stood back; Shult and Kerch entered the room. Hetzel said, "Allow me to introduce my guest, Vv. Gidion Dirby."

Shult refused to acknowledge the introduction. Kerch gave Dirby an uninterested nod. "I am here in connection with Vv. Dirby," said Shult. "Unfortunately, I must ask him to depart the premises at once."

"This is a curious demand," said Hetzel.

"Not at all. I have received notice to the effect that Vv. Dirby has committed a serious crime, namely, the assassination of two dignitaries. The Beyranion cannot function as a sanctuary for criminals."

"Vv. Dirby does not fit this description," said Hetzel. "He tells me that he is innocent of wrongdoing. Furthermore, he is not a casual intruder upon the premises; he is here as my guest."

Shult's face became obdurate. "Captain Baw of the Gaean Security Force has made a specific statement. He identifies Vv. Dirby as the assassin."

"This is more puzzling than ever. Captain Baw told me that he merely heard the shots. Who made the identification?"

"Captain Baw vouchsafed no details."

"But details are the gist of the matter. Several other persons were present when the assassinations occurred, including three Gomaz, two of whom were killed."

"I cannot judge any of this," said Shult. "Captain Baw is waiting in my office; he insists that I expel Vv. Dirby into his custody."

"You would thereby set a very dangerous precedent," said Hetzel. "Do you want Captain Baw appearing every few days to demand one or another of your guests, who for some reason or another has annoyed the Triarchs? or the Liss authorities? Or the Olefract? They have rights equal and equivalent to Captain Baw."

Kerch said, "Vv. Hetzel is quite right on this score."

Shult pursed his lips. "Naturally, I want nothing of the sort. Still, my responsibility extends only to patrons of the hotel."

"I have already pointed out that Vv. Dirby is my guest."

"He is not registered as such."

"That is irrelevant. I have rented a suite of rooms, not a single occupancy; I have the right to entertain as many guests as I wish. Now, there is another point that you have not considered. The Triskelion is a special entity, and not subject to Gaean law. The Beyranion Hotel is very definitely subject to Gaean law. Vv. Dirby has been proved guilty of nothing. If you irresponsibly turn him over to Captain Baw, and should he thereby suffer harm, you are liable for damages and a punitive fine, perhaps ten or twenty million SLU. You are treading upon exceedingly thin legal ice."

Shult now exhibited signs of nervousness. He glanced at Kerch, who merely shrugged and turned away. "This is all very well, but I still cannot allow myself to harbor an assassin."

"Who says he is an assassin?"

"Well . . . Captain Baw."

"I suggest that you ask Captain Baw to assemble his witnesses and his evidence and bring everything here, and then we can decide upon Vv. Dirby's guilt or innocence. Even then, you are not obliged to respond. We stand on Gaean territory; yonder is a joint jurisdiction of three races, two of whom are alien. Under no circumstances can you allow yourself to be intimidated by Captain Baw."

Aeolus Shult heaved a deep sigh. "There is something in what you say. We must always act with due regard for Gaean justice." He gave Hetzel a doleful salute and departed, followed by Kerch.

After several moments Dirby spoke. "So . . . I'm a prisoner at the Beyranion."

"Until you prove yourself innocent."

Dirby lapsed into mulish silence. Fifteen minutes passed. The telephone chimed. Hetzel touched the audio button. The screen lit up to display the tea-rose delicacy of Sir Estevan's blond receptionist. "Hetzel speaking."

"This is the office of the Gaean Triarch. Sir Estevan Tristo regrets that he was unable to meet with you earlier today; however, he is free now and requests that you call at his office."

"Now?"

"If it is convenient."

Hetzel reflected a moment. "Please connect me with Sir Estevan."

"Just a minute, sir. Will you be good enough to press your video button?"

"When Sir Estevan comes on."

"Very good, sir."

The screen brightened, to show a keen-featured face. Dirby came forward and stared intently at the image. He nodded to Hetzel. "That's Handsome."

Hetzel touched the video button. Sir Estevan said, "You are Vv. Miro Hetzel, who called at the Triskelion earlier today?"

"Quite correct, sir."

"I would be pleased to see you now, if you are at liberty."

"That is kind of you. However, another matter must be taken into consideration."

"You refer to Gidion Dirby?"

Hetzel nodded. "I would like to call on you, but I do not care to be seized as soon as I leave the Beyranion and held on some trumped-up charge. If this is to be the case, I would prefer that you came here to see me."

Sir Estevan smiled a wintry smile. "Let me check with the commandant."

The screen went blank. Hetzel switched off the audio and looked at Dirby. "So that's Handsome."

Dirby nodded. "His hair is different. He wears it more formally."

"What of his voice?"

Dirby hesitated. "It's somewhat different. Considerably different, in fact."

"Has it occurred to you that on the two occasions you saw Handsome at close hand he wore first a veil and then a morion that concealed a good part of his face? On the other occasions, he stood in a doorway in a section of wall where no doorway existed."

"What are you suggesting?"

"That your experience of Handsome for the most part was a projected image, and that the voice might or might not have been his own."

Dirby scowled. "So that Handsome wasn't out there at all."

"It seems that diligent efforts were made to arouse your antagonism against Sir Estevan."

Dirby laughed. "Then they bring me here to the Triskelion, give me a dead zap, and show me Sir Estevan. Why all this?"

"Two Triarchs were killed—an Olefract and a Liss. It would be more difficult to arouse animosity against these two."

Dirby shook his head. "I don't understand it."

"I don't understand it either," said Hetzel. "You call him Handsome. I call him Casimir Wuldfache."

Sir Estevan returned to the screen. Hetzel restored the sound. "I have conferred with Captain Baw," said Sir Estevan. "Understandably, he is anxious for information."

"All of us share this anxiety, including Gidion Dirby. For instance, he would like to know why you turned a pot of ordure over his head."

Sir Estevan Tristo raised his eyebrows. He reached out and made an adjustment on the clarity control. "I don't believe I heard your remarks correctly."

"No matter," said Hetzel. "I want only your assurance that if I leave the hotel I won't be subjected to inconvenience."

"If you transgress our laws, or if you have done so, you will face the ordinary consequences. However, Captain Baw tells me that to the best of his knowledge you have committed no such acts."

"I then have your explicit assurance that I will not be arrested?"

"Not unless you commit a crime."

"Very well," said Hetzel. "I'll risk it."

CHAPTER 7

Hetzel set off across the Plaza toward the murky outline of the Triskelion. He observed no persons in the blue-and-green uniform of the Gaean Security Patrol, and when he arrived at the Triskelion, the officer on duty paid him no extraordinary attention. Captain Baw was not in evidence.

Hetzel approached the Gaean section of the reception desk. The Liss and Olefract sides of the triangle, as usual, were vacant. Vv. Kylo, who was on duty alone, directed Hetzel to a door across the lobby. Hetzel entered an antechamber where Sir Estevan's pretty blond receptionist sat at a desk. The telephone image failed to do justice to the girl. Her coloring, thought Hetzel, was exquisite—pale-blond hair like winter sunlight, flower-petal skin, features delicate, almost over-refined, as if she derived from generations of aesthetes and aristocrats. For Hetzel's taste she was perhaps too sensitive, too fastidious and meticulous, and perhaps humorless as well; nevertheless, she added a great deal of tone to Sir Estevan's office.

"Vv. Hetzel? This way, please."

Sir Estevan arose from his desk to meet Hetzel—a man tall and stern, but undeniably handsome. He was, thought Hetzel, older than Casimir Wuldfache. The resemblance, though strong, dissipated somewhat upon close inspection.

Sir Estevan indicated a chair, and seated himself. "You are an almost obsessively cautious man."

"Captain Baw's zeal compels such an obsession," said Hetzel.

Sir Estevan allowed himself a faint smile. "I think you referred to Gidion Dirby as your client?"

"By no means. His situation interests me, and I am acting informally as his adviser. He is not my client. The distinction is important."

"You were previously acquainted?"

"I met him for the first time today. His predicament attracted my attention, and the story he tells aroused my professional interest.'

"I see. May I inquire your profession?"

"I am an effectuator, of a specialized sort—in fact, something of a dilettante. I rescue distressed maidens, I undertake interesting missions, I search for lost fortunes."

"In which of these categories does Gidion Dirby fit?"

"He is hardly a maiden in distress," said Hetzel. "Nonetheless, I am attempting to protect him from his enemies."

Sir Estevan laughed his chilly laugh. "And who protects the enemies against Gidion Dirby?"

"I wish to discuss this matter with you. First, do you believe Gidion Dirby to be the assassin?"

"I see no other possibility, nor does Captain Baw. Consult him; he was much closer to the action."

"You did not observe Dirby shoot his gun?"

"No. Captain Baw obscured my view. I heard the sound of the pellets; I saw two Gomaz killed, and dropped behind my desk. Essentially, I saw nothing of what happened."

"You never saw Vv. Dirby at all?"

"Not clearly."

"Did you recognize him when you saw his face in the view plate?"

"No, he is a stranger to me."

"Why should he—or anyone else, for that matter—attempt to assassinate the Triarchs?"

Sir Estevan leaned back in his chair. "I assume that the murderer was and is insane. There is no other explanation. The deed is absolutely pointless."

"What if the surviving Gomaz were the assassin?"

Sir Estevan shook his head. "It is not the nature of the Gomaz to assassinate. He kills for his own private reasons—'lusts' might be the applicable word; otherwise, he is neither violent nor murderous, unless he is molested."

"You have apparently made a close study of the Gomaz."

"Naturally; why else am I here?"

"The Liss and the Olefract share your interest?"

Sir Estevan shrugged. "We have little communication between us. Certainly no informal contacts. The Liss are suspicious and hostile; the Olefract are contemptuous and hostile. But still no reason to kill their Triarchs."

"And how will they react?"

"Reasonably enough, or so I imagine. If Dirby is deranged, they'll accept the killing as an aberrated act."

"Assuming that Dirby is indeed the killer."

"There's no other possibility."

"Captain Baw was in the chamber."

"Ridiculous. Why should he perform such an act?"

"Why should Gidion Dirby?"

"Insanity."

"Perhaps Baw is insane."

"Rubbish."

Hetzel indicated a door. "This leads into the Triarchic chamber?"

"It does."

"Your receptionist at all times had the door under observation?"

"She certainly would have noticed someone standing here shooting at me."

"Perhaps someone was hidden in the chamber?"

"Impossible. I was fifteen minutes early into the chamber. No one was hidden there."

"Well, then . . . what about yourself?"

Sir Estevan showed his cold smile. "I'd prefer to fix the guilt on Gidion Dirby, or the Gomaz, or even Baw, for that matter."

"And the Gomaz—why were they here?"

"They had no opportunity to explain themselves."

"Won't this assassination cause problems? Raids? Demonstrations?"

"Probably not. The Gomaz are linked telepathically to the unitary consciousness of their sept, and they are not disturbed by death. This is an element of their ferocity." Sir Estevan tossed a pamphlet across his desk. "Read this, if you're interested in the Gomaz."

"Thank you." The pamphlet was entitled *The Gomaz Warriors of SJZ-BEA-1545 (Maz), Prepared by the Hannenborg Institute for Xenological Research*. He inspected the diagram on the cover. "Two hundred and twenty-nine septs. The Gomaz who visited you this morning—what was their sept?"

"Ubiakh." Sir Estevan gave his fingers an impatient twitch. "Surely you did not come here to discuss the Gomaz?"

Hetzel opened his mouth to mention Istagam, then had second thoughts. It might be wise to secure an air-car-use permit for reasons other than investigating Istagam. "At the moment, I am preoccupied with Gidion Dirby and his extraordinary plight."

"What is so extraordinary about it?"

"I would like you to hear Gidion Dirby's story from his own mouth. Could you step over to the Beyranion for a few minutes?"

"I'd prefer that you give me the gist of it here."

"Gidion Dirby declares that he was held captive and subjected to a number of fantastic tricks; you were the chief trickmaster, and terminated the proceedings by turning a chamber pot over his head."

Sir Estevan grinned. "I deny this."

"You have never seen Gidion Dirby previous to to-day?"

"Never, to my knowledge."

"Are you familiar with a long enclosed corridor with white tile walls and a high white ceiling?"

"Possibly. Such a corridor connects the loggia of my residence to the morning room. Why do you ask?"

"This hall figures in Gidion Dirby's account, and it tends to authenticate his story."

Sir Estevan considered. "If Dirby is innocent, then either I or Captain Baw must be guilty of murder. Or conceivably my secretary, Zaressa, if your imagination can cope with the image of her standing in that doorway and gunning down a Liss, an Olefract, and two Gomaz."

"If Dirby is innocent, then you, Captain Baw, Zaressa, or the Gomaz must be guilty. I agree to this."

"It would be most tiresome," said Sir Estevan, "especially since the Gomaz must be removed from the list. Far better that an addle-brained zealot be declared the assassin, whether he is guilty, as I believe him to be, or not."

"Dirby might concede this point of view," said Hetzel, "if he were granted safe-conduct away from Maz and recompensed for his inconvenience. At the moment, he is annoyed and unhappy, and he is anxious to bring the facts to light."

"This, of course, is his option. How does he propose to perform the illumination?"

"The Gomaz was present; why not question him?"

Sir Estevan leaned back in his chair and pondered. "Gomaz make poor witnesses. They are unresponsive—contemptuously unresponsive, I should say—to our laws and customs. They will say what they wish to say, and no more. It is impossible to coerce a Gomaz, and it is also impossible to appeal, shall we say, to his better nature."

"Incidentally, what was their business with the Triarchy?"

"Before a statement could be made, the assassinations occurred."

Hetzel thought to detect evasiveness. "Did they not state their business for your agenda?"

"No." Sir Estevan's reply was curt.

"And you yourself do not know what their business might have been?"

"I would not care to speculate."

"From Dirby's point of view, the surviving Gomaz is a prime witness. It would seem that if a Gomaz testified at all, he would speak the truth."

"The truth as he saw it. By no means the truth as we see it."

"Still, in all fairness, we should hear what he has to tell us."

Sir Estevan hesitated a moment, then took up a schedule, which he studied a moment. He punched a button on his telephone. The screen became bright; a face looked forth; a voice spoke. "Maz Transport. Yes, Sir Estevan."

"Has the Route Five carrier left on schedule?"

"Yes, sir, half an hour ago."

"How many passengers were aboard?"

"One moment sir. . . . Seven passengers: two

Kaikash, two Ironbellies, a Ubaikh, an Aqzh, and a Yellow Hellion."

"Look out into the corral. Do you see any Ubaikh?"

"It's empty, sir. Everyone left on the transport."

"Thank you." Sir Estevan switched off the screen. "The Gomaz has returned to his castle, and must be considered inaccessible."

"Not necessarily. I can be on hand when the carrier puts him down, and interview him there."

"Hmmf." Sir Estevan studied Hetzel a long ten seconds. "How will you communicate with him?"

"You must have a suitable translator."

"Naturally. A valuable piece of equipment."

"I'll post bond on it, if you wish."

"That's not necessary. Zaressa will get it for you. You can rent an air car from the tourist agency in Dogtown." He scribbled a note, handed it to Hetzel. "That's your permit. They'll send one of their personnel with you; that's our invariable rule, to keep inexperienced people out of trouble. Maz is a dangerous planet, and naturally you go out at your own risk. The agency man will know how to find the Ubaikh depot. Don't go hear the castle; they'll kill you. At the depot you're safe enough." He looked at the schedule. "You've got ample time. The carrier won't arrive at Ubaikh until tomorrow afternoon. I'll want to look over the tape of the interview; is that understood?"

"Certainly. Now, one other matter . . ."

Sir Estevan glanced at his watch. "I'm a bit pressed for time."

"I came here to Maz to inquire about Istagam, as the concern is known. My principals are concerned by Istagam's low prices; they fear that the Liss and the Olefract are using Maz as a port of entry from which to flood the Gaean markets."

Sir Estevan's lip curled. "You can assure them otherwise. Neither Liss nor Olefract want contact with the Gaeans, or with each other."

"Then who or what is Istagam?"

Sir Estevan spoke almost primly. "I have heard the word mentioned, and I believe that there is no illegality involved. You may so inform your principals, and they will have to trim their sails to the wind."

"Can you identify the directors of Istagam, or tell me anything about their mode of operation?"

"I'm sorry, sir; this is a matter that I can't discuss."

"On what grounds?"

"Caprice," said Sir Estevan. "That's as good a reason as any. I'm sorry that I now must terminate our discussion."

Hetzel rose to his feet. "Thank you for your courtesy. It has been a pleasure talking with you."

"Bring me back the translator tape; I'll want to check it over."

"I'll be sure to do so."

Captain Baw stood three inches taller than Hetzel; his shoulders, chest, and abdomen bulged with muscle; his round, flat face was cold and wary. He rose briskly to his feet when Hetzel entered his office, and stood sternly erect during the period of the interview.

"You are Captain Baw, I believe."

"I am he."

"Sir Estevan suggested that I consult you, in order to clarify exactly what happened this morning."

"Very good, then, consult away."

"You were present when the killings occurred?"

"I was indeed."

"What was the precise sequence of events?"

"I brought in a man named Gidion Dirby, who claimed urgent business with Sir Estevan. As I stepped forward to attract Sir Estevan's attention, he produced a gun and opened fire."

"You saw him shoot the gun?"

"He stood behind me, from where the shots originated."

"What of the Gomaz? They stood behind you as well."

"Gomaz are not allowed to carry guns."

"Assume that through some unusual circumstance, one of the Gomaz did in fact carry a gun—what then?"

"First: he would not kill in cold blood. Second: he would not kill his fellows. Third: he would not depart without making a thorough job of it."

"What happened to the weapon?"

"I have no information in this regard. You must put the question to Gidion Dirby."

"As a matter of fact, I have done so. Somewhat to his surprise, he did find a gun in his pocket. The cells were discharged and the contacts were corroded. The gun has not been fired for months. What do you say to that?"

In a voice of long-suffering patience, Captain Baw replied, "Sir, it is not my place to argue with you. Ask your questions of fact; I will respond as well as I can."

"You state that you did not actually see the gun being fired."

Baw lowered his eyelids, and his eyes became such narrow lines of leaden gristle that Hetzel wondered how he could see. "I will merely assert, sir, that the shots came from the vicinity of Gidion Dirby. I glimpsed the action from the corner of my eye; I was somewhat preoccupied with the Gomaz, who had become restless and upset."

"Why did you not immediately rush forth and capture Gidion Dirby?"

"My first dity was to Sir Estevan. I assured myself that he was not seriously hurt, and had a brief discussion with him. Then, when I went to seek Vv. Dirby, he was

nowhere to be seen. I assumed that he had taken himself
to Far Dogtown, where we lack jurisdiction."

"You might have caught him, had you hurried."

"Perhaps so, sir, but there was no basis on which I
might have arrested him, and this was the subject of my
discussion with Sir Estevan. Dirby's shots killed a Liss
in Liss territory, an Olefract in Olefract territory, and no
one has bothered to pass a law against killing Gomaz.
The shoe is on the other foot. We have no formal ex-
tradition procedures with either Liss or Olefract, nor
have they as yet made any representations to us."

"All this seems highly abstract," said Hetzel. "I
would expect that when you observe a man killing two
Triarchs, you would capture him first and worry about
charges later."

Baw condescended a small smile. "This procedure
might be feasible within the Reach. You do not understand how carefully we must deal with the Liss and
Olefract. We adhere to the exact letter of our contract;
they do the same with us. Only in this way can we ac-
commodate each other."

"So, then, what is Dirby's status as of this moment?"

"We have issued a complaint of misdemeanor against
Gidion Dirby, asserting that he fired weapons during
official proceedings of the Triarchy and disrupted the
session."

"This is not the statement you made to Aeolus Shult,
at the Beyranion."

"At the Beyranion I have no official status. I can use
unofficial language and perform unofficial acts, such as
laying hold of Dirby and dragging him out on the Plaza
to where I could arrest him."

"On misdemeanor charges?"

"Exactly."

"What is the penalty for such an offense?"

"He must be adjudged."

"By whom?"

"In connection with small crimes, I generally act as magistrate."

"And how do you adjudge Gidion Dirby?"

"Guilty."

"And his penalty?"

Captain Baw's thinking had not proceeded so far. "I must consult the statutes."

"Why not do so now? I will pay the fine."

Captain Baw made a brusque gesture. "If you think to pay some trifling sum in Gidion Dirby's name and win him away free and guiltless, you are mistaken."

"You have done this much yourself."

Captain Baw's mouth became a loose O of indignant astonishment. "How so?"

"You have tried and adjudged him of firing shots in the Triarchy chamber, and found him guilty. Regardless of his guilt or innocence, a man may not be twice held to account for the same charges."

Captain Baw's face began to turn pink. He spoke in a heavy voice. "This interpretation will not carry weight, I assure you."

"I thought not," said Hetzel.

"There may be an additional charge, such as felonious attack upon the life of Sir Estevan Tristo."

"How can this be? Only four shots were fired, and four individuals were killed!" This remark was casual essay; Hetzel had no notion whatever as to how many shots had been fired.

"The number of shots fired is not germane," said Baw laboriously. "Gidion Dirby must surrender himself at once, or seriously compromise his position."

"I will tell him so," said Hetzel, "and I thank you for your courtesy. But one more matter puzzles me. I identified the Gomaz as Kaikash—"

"Kaikash? Nonsense. They were Ubaikh. Kaikash

wear a peaked helmet and black leggings, and they smell different. I can't read the smells so that I know what they mean, but I can tell a Kaikash from a Ubaikh."

"What did they want from the Triarchs?"

"The matter lies beyond my province."

"But you know?"

"Of course I know. It is my business to know everything."

"Sir Estevan declared that you would answer all questions freely."

"In my opinion, Sir Estevan is far too liberal. There is no reason why we should explain official business to every astounded tourist. I will say this much: the Ubaikh consider themselves an elite. They led all the septs in the great war, and now they hold themselves first among the Gomaz, and they are always the first to complain of any and every fancied encroachment."

"I would consider Istagam more than an encroachment," said Hetzel. "No reasonable man could say otherwise."

Captain Baw looked off across the room. "In this regard, there can be no discussion."

"It is foolish to ignore a notorious reality," said Hetzel.

"Not all that notorious," grumbled Captain Baw. "A trivial matter, really."

"Then why should the Ubaikh come here to complain?"

"I don't know, and I don't care!" roared Captain Baw. "I can talk no more today!"

"Thank you, Captain Baw."

CHAPTER 8

Hetzel found Gidion Dirby sitting on a hummock of purple-black moss in that corner of the garden overlooking Dogtown. He seemed morose and preoccupied and when Hetzel approached, he turned a resentful glance over his shoulder. Gidion Dirby, thought Hetzel, was not a likable man. Still, he must be excused a certain degree of peevishness. After similar treatment, Hetzel might also become misanthropic.

Dirby asked, "Well . . . did you see Sir Estevan?"

"Yes, He told me nothing we don't already know. I also spoke to Captain Baw, who seems somewhat uncertain. He tells me that the deed for which you are held liable is a simple misdemeanor. The Triarchs have never established a mutually binding legal code; no one trusts anyone else, and each party enforces its own laws upon its own subjects. Gaean interest in the missiles that killed the Liss and the Olefract ends as soon as those missiles cross the lines of jurisdiction. Killing Gomaz is not yet illegal. Hence, even had you shot the gun, your offense is simple disorderly conduct. This is the theory. In effect, Sir Estevan might informally extradite you to the Liss or the Olefract. Though this I somehow doubt. He is a complex man, a puzzling man. He seems very confident."

Dirby gave an inarticulate growl. "They purposely allowed me to escape, because they couldn't risk a public trial, with mind-search evidence."

"I'm sure of nothing," said Hetzel. "Sir Estevan tells me that there is a long blue-and-white-tiled hall in his residence. Someone photographed him walking along this hall and adapted the film to your situation. . . . I neglected to ask who might have so filmed him."

"And when he turned the pot over my head—that was also a photograph?"

"That might not have been Sir Estevan. In fact, almost certainly it was Casimir Wuldfache."

Dirby rose to his feet and stood rubbing his chin. "If my offense is just simple misdemeanor, why not go over to the Triskelion and pay a fee?"

"It's not quite that simple. Captain Baw comprises the whole legal system in himself. He might sentence you to thirty lashes, or eighteen years in the Exhibitory, or expulsion into Liss territory. You had better remain at the Beyranion until you have legal counsel and a Gaean marshal on the job."

"That will be a month, or maybe two months."

"Do as you like," said Hetzel. "Shall I continue the investigation?"

"I suppose you might as well."

"If you turn yourself in, I'm going to stop. I can't collect money from a dead man."

Dirby only grunted.

Hetzel drew a deep breath and went on. "We've only scratched the surface of this case. Right now, at least, several matters seem important. Where is Banghart? Where is Casimir Wuldfache? Where were you confined? Is your case linked with Istagam? If so, how?"

"Don't ask me," said Dirby. "I'm just the turkey."

"Does Banghart have other names or a Gaean index by which he might be traced?"

"Not to my knowledge."

"What does he look like?"

Dirby scratched his chin. "He's older than I; stocky, with a square face and black hair. He doesn't seem particularly impressive until he gives you orders and looks at you. He's cold inside. He likes to dress well; in fact, he's something of a dandy. He spoke once or twice of a place called Fallorne."

"Fallorne is a world on the other side of the Reach. Anything else?"

"He had a strange way of singing. I can't quite describe it—as if singing two tunes at once, a kind of counterpoint. I can't think of much else."

"Very good. Now, you were put down on a swampy island. Do you remember the weather?"

"It was just an ordinary clear night."

"Could you see stars?"

"Not distinctly. The air blurs them out, and the moon was stark full, which concealed even more stars."

"How high did the moon rise above the horizon? In other words, what was its maximum height in degrees?"

Dirby shrugged peevishly. "I hardly noticed. I wasn't concerned with astronomical observations. Let me think. I don't believe it went higher than about forty-five degrees—halfway up the sky. Don't ask me about the sun, because I didn't notice; in fact, I hardly saw it."

"Very well, but you noticed where the sun rose?"

Dirby allowed himself a sour smile. "In the east."

"In the east is correct. Now, then, on the night previously, did the moon climb the northern sky or the southern sky?"

"The southern sky. But what difference does all this make?"

"Any information might be useful. In the room where you were held, did you notice any indication of the passing days? Any difference between night and day?"

"No."

"But you think you were held prisoner two or three months."

"About that. I don't really know."

"You never heard sounds outside your room? Conversation?"

"Nothing. Never."

"If you think of anything," said Hetzel, "make a note of it."

Dirby started to speak, then held his tongue. Hetzel watched him a moment. Perhaps his adventure had, for a fact, distorted his thinking processes. His perceptions must have been honed; he would experience events in terms of contrasts and extremes. All colors would seem saturated; all voices would ring with both truth and duplicity; all acts would seem pregnant with mysterious symbolism. In a certain sense, Dirby must be regarded as irresponsible. Hetzel spoke in an even voice. "Remember, do not leave the grounds of the hotel; in fact, you would be wise to stay indoors."

Dirby's reply confirmed his suspicions. "Wisdom doesn't work as well as you might imagine."

"Everything else works much worse," said Hetzel. "I have some business in Dogtown, and I'll be gone for an hour or two, or perhaps the rest of the afternoon. I suggest, first, that you rayogram your father, then sit quietly somewhere. Talk to the tourists. Relax. Sleep. Above all, don't do anything to get yourself kicked out of the hotel."

From the rear of the Beyranion Hotel a flight of rock-melt steps zigzagged down the face of a sandstone bluff, to join the road connecting the space depot and Far Dogtown. Hetzel had not yet visited this district southeast of Dogtown proper, in Gomaz territory and outside the Gaean Reach. This was the Dogtown of popular

imagination, the so-called City of Nameless Men. Every
other building appeared to be an inn of greater or lesser
pretension, each stridently asserting its vitality with a
sign or a standard, painted, sometimes crudely, sometimes artfully, in colors that gave zest to structures built
of drab stone from the bluff, or planks of local
wormwood, or slabs sawed from burls.

The time was now late afternoon; the folk of Far
Dogtown had come forth to take a draft of beer, or a
flask of wine, or a dram of spirits, at rude tables before
taverns or under the acacias that grew down the center
of the street. They sat alone or in small groups of twos
and threes, talking in confidential mumbles punctuated
with an occasional guffaw or a jocular curse, eyeing each
passerby with stony, speculative gazes. Hetzel recognized garments and trinkets from half a hundred worlds.
Here sat a man with hair in varnished ringlets after the
fasion of Arbonetta; there sat another with the cropped
ears of a Destrinary. This man with the slantwise velvet
cap and the dangle of black pearls past his ear might be
a starmenter from Alastor Cluster, what could bring
him so far across the galaxy?

And those two girls, sisters or twins, with pale snub-
nose faces and orange hair; they seemed very young to
be so far from Marmonfyre. But most of the folk taking
their ease at the taverns of Far Dogtown wore garments
much like those of Hetzel himself—the unobtrusive
dress of the galactic wanderer, who preferred to attract
a minimum of attention.

The street took a jog and widened by a few yards; here
was a cluster of small shops: food-markets; a pharmacy
and dispensary; a haberdasher with racks of ready-to-
wear garments and crates of boots, shoes, and sandals;
a newsstand with journals from various sections of the
Reach. . . . Hetzel felt a sudden uneasy pang. Halting to
study an offering of fraudulent identification papers and
packets of counterfeit money, he managed to glance

back the way he had come, but the man following him, if such there were, had stepped into a public urinal.

Hetzel continued. His instincts were right more often than not, and if he were indeed being trailed, the fact should come as no surprise. Hetzel was nonetheless displeased. To be followed elsewhere in the Reach might indicate simple curiosity; in Far Dogtown, such attention might mean death.

The road passed under a wooden archway; Far Dogtown became Dogtown, where Gaean law prevailed. Hetzel proceeded to the central square, and paused again to look behind him. Nothing, except the street and a few individuals out upon their errands. Hetzel strolled around the square and proceeded past the office of tourist information, to a shop offering Gomaz boneware for sale. He sidled quickly into the dim interior. He could not be certain, but a dark form might have stepped into the acacia grove that occupied the center of the square.

The proprietor approached—a frail old man in a white smock with lens cups over his eyes. "What would you care to examine, sir?"

"These bowls here—what is their worth?"

"Aha! These are adult Zoum skulls, with palladium rims and a palladium foot. Excellent craftsmanship, as you can see. The material is as dense as stone, and of course has been carefully cleaned and sterilized. Think what a conversation you'll have when you serve your guests their broth! The price for a dozen is a hundred and fifty SLU."

"A bit more than I care to pay," said Hetzel. "Can't I outrage my guests more cheaply?"

"Well, yes, of course. These ladles are fashioned from the skulls of Voulash bantlings. Their play wars are as deadly as the efforts of the adults, as perhaps you know."

No one had emerged from the acacia grove. Hetzel

disliked such uncertainty. The ambience of Far Dogtown no doubt had stimulated him to hypersensitivity.

". . . back scratchers are the shins and toes of very young bantlings, a clever and unusual article."

"Thank you. I will keep your recommendations in mind." Hetzel gave the square a last inspection. He stepped forth and walked to the office of tourist information.

At the counter stood the same young woman to whom he had spoken previously. Today she wore breeches of beige velvet gathered at the ankles, a dark-brown jacket with gold brocade, a gold fillet to confine her dark hair. Hetzel thought that she recognized him, but her voice was institutionally polite. "Yes, sir, can I be of help?"

"Are you able to produce an astronomical almanac?"

"An astronomical almanac, sir?"

"Any information relating to the movement of the sun, the moon, and Maz in their orbits should be sufficient."

"This little calendar shows the phases of the moon. Will that help you?"

"I'm afraid not." Hetzel gave the sketch a cursory glance. "Just a minute; let me reconsider. The plane of the orbit of the moon appears to cut the plane of Maz's orbit at right angles."

"Yes; it's quite unusual, so I'm told."

In such a case, Hetzel reflected, the moon would be at full when it crossed the plane of Maz's orbit directly behind Maz in relation to the sun. Hetzel checked the calendar and noted the date of this occurrence. On this date, Gidion Dirby had sat on a swamp island with the moon approximately halfway up the southern sky. Since the moon at this instant had been very close to the plane of Maz's orbit, the latitude of the swamp island would be approximately 45° North, plus or minus the tilt of the ecliptic plane.

"Perhaps," said Hetzel, "you have a reference book that might provide general information in regard to Maz?"

The girl produced a pamphlet. "If you explained what you wanted to know, I might provide the answer."

"You might," said Hetzel, "but more likely not. Let me see, now. The Maz year is 441 days, each of 21.74 standard hours. The plane of rotation is inclined twelve degrees to the plane of the ecliptic . . ." Hetzel returned to the calendar. "What is considered the middle of summer and the middle of winter?"

"We don't have much of either. It's mostly a wet season in summer and a dry season in winter. It's now fall, and we're well into the dry period, lucky for you. When it rains, it rains a torrent. The calendar uses the standard month names—only here the months are ten days longer than they were at home on Varsilla."

"Varsilla! The world of nine blue oceans and ten thousand sea peaks and eleven million islands."

"And twelve billion sand flies and sixteen billion glass nettles, and twenty billion tourist villas. So you know Varsilla?"

"Not well."

"Have you visited Palestria on Jailand?"

"I never had occasion to leave Meyness."

"That's a pity; Jailand is so beautiful and placid. Too placid, I used to think. But I wish I were there now. I'm bored with Maz. Anyway, Iulian is summer there, and summer here. The months naturally don't come at the same time."

Hetzel studied the calendar. The summer solstice occurred about the first day of Iulian. It appeared, then, that the moon had reached full almost exactly at the autumnal equinox. Hence there would be neither subtraction nor addition of degrees, and the swamp island, if Dirby's estimate were accurate, must be found somewhere near latitude 45° North.

The girl was watching Hetzel curiously. "Have you reached an important decision?" Her mouth showed an impish twitch.

"So!" said Hetzel. "You consider me solemn and foolish!"

"Of course not! I never think thus of tourists!"

Hetzel merely raised his eyebrows. "Can you show me a large scale map of Maz, preferably a Mercator projection?"

"Of course." She touched a dial and pressed a button; on the hard white surface of the wall appeared a map as tall as Hetzel and twelve feet wide. "Is that satisfactory?"

"Excellent. Where is Dogtown?"

The girl put her finger on the map. "Here." She looked over her shoulder. "Excuse me a moment." She went back to the desk to deal with a pair of tourists in white suits and wide-brimmed white hats with souvenir emblems pinned to the ribbons.

"Where can we see the Gomaz warriors in a real battle?" asked the man. "I'm hoping to get some shots for a travelogue."

The girl smiled politely. "Battles aren't all that easy. The Gomaz refuse to keep us informed. Very churlish of them, of course."

"Oh, dear," said the woman. "We promised everyone we'd bring back films. I understand we're not allowed in the tribal castles?"

"I'm afraid that is so. But we've remodeled a number of ancient castles into very comfortable inns, which I'm told are very typical. I've never visited one myself."

"Can't you arrange to find a battle for us? I very much wanted to film an authentic Gomaz war."

The girl smilingly shook her head. "You'd probably be killed if you ventured that close."

"Where would you say we have the best chance of seeing a good battle?"

"I don't know what a good one would be like," said the girl, "or a bad one either, for that matter. It's probably just a matter of luck—'misfortune' might be a better word, because these affairs are very dangerous."

Hetzel found latitude 45° North. He traced it over oceans, mountains, uplands, and moors. A thousand miles north of Axistil, a river flowing down from the northern moors wandered out upon a flatland and dissipated into a thousand trickles and rills. This was the Great Kykh-Kych Swamp. Hetzel inspected it carefully. Nearby, he noticed a black dot.

The tourists departed. A door from the adjoining office opened, and a burly man looked forth—Byrrhis. Today he wore a modish suit of dark-green twill, with a black-and-scarlet cravat. "Janika, I'm leaving for the day. Transfer my calls to my villa."

"Yes, Vv. Byrrhis."

"Mind you, lock up well. Don't forget the back windows."

"Yes, Vv. Byrrhis, I'll be careful."

Byrrhis gave Hetzel a friendly nod, which might or might not have connoted recognition. He retreated into his office, evidently planning to leave by a different exit.

Hetzel asked, "What did he call you?"

"Janika."

"Is that your name?"

"It's short for my girl-name, which most people consider rather queer—Lljiano. Two L's sounded on your side teeth. It's an old Hiulak name."

"I didn't know the Hiulaks settled on Varsilla."

"They didn't. My father's name is Reyes; he's part Maljin and part White Drasthanyi. He met my mother on Fanuche and brought her back to Varsilla. And she's a quarter Semiric, which makes me something of a mongrel."

"A very healthy looking mongrel."

"Where are you from?"

"I was born on Old Earth. My name is Miro Hetzel. I am told that I come of decadent stock because all the enterprising persons long ago immigrated to the stars."

"You don't seem decadent; you seem quite ordinary."

"I'm sure you intend a compliment."

"Of a sort." Janika laughed. "Did you find what you were looking for?"

"I think so. What are these red stars?"

"They're the sites of the touristic inns—all picturesque and comfortable, so I'm told. I've never visited any of them."

"And what is this black circle?"

"You'll see several of them on the map. They're ruins that are especially quaint, where Vv. Byrrhis wants to establish new inns."

"The others do well?"

"Moderately well. Lots of tourists insist upon a Gomaz war, which we can't produce. Of course, we've never tried, but I doubt if the Gomaz would take kindly to the idea."

"The Gomaz are a humorless lot. I understand that I can rent an air car through this office."

"It's the only agency in Dogtown. You must have a clearance from Sir Estevan Tristo, and you must be accompanied by an official guide, to prevent you from smuggling weapons or selling the air car."

"I have the clearance, and also a good idea. Why don't you come along as the official guide?"

"Me? I couldn't stop you from smuggling weapons."

"That's a restriction I'll agree to right now—no smuggling."

"Well . . . it sounds pleasant. When did you have in mind?"

"Tomorrow."

"I'm supposed to work tomorrow, but that's no real problem. A substitute could take over. Where did you plan to go?"

"Oh, I don't know. Off in this direction, I suppose; we could have lunch at this inn."

"That's Black Cliff Castle, which is supposed to be very dramatic. But it's a long way off." She glanced sidewise at Hetzel. "It's actually more than a one-day trip."

"All the better. Book a couple of rooms for us, then we won't need to rush. Are you doubtful? Of your job? Or of me?"

" 'Doubt' is not quite the word." Janika laughed rather nervously.

"Caution? Apprehension?"

"No, none of these. . . . Oh, well, why not? I haven't been out of Dogtown in all the time I've been here. Vv. Byrrhis can fire me if he wants; I don't really care."

"How long have you worked here?"

"Only three months, and just about ready to think 'why not?' again and go back to Varsilla."

"Is Vv. Byrrhis so harsh a taskmaster?"

"He has his crotchets." Janika put on as prim and stern an expression as her features were capable of forming. "I must insist that I pay my own expenses."

"Just as you like," said Hetzel. "The only person to profit will be a certain Sir Ivon Hacaway, who can well bear the expense."

Hetzel returned to the Plaza by way of the Avenue of Lost Souls. The time was early evening; the sky swam with violet and pale-green murk. He crossed the dim Plaza to the Beyranion Hotel, and found Dirby in the lobby, sitting quietly in a lounge chair with a journal. Dirby looked up with mingled suspicion and curiosity. "What have you learned in Dogtown?"

Hetzel evaded the question. "You've never been there?"

"When I was here on the *Tarinthia* I went down for an evening or two. I've seen better places."

Hetzel nodded agreement. "Still, there's a special atmosphere to Dogtown: vain regrets, lost causes—they hang in the air like smoke.''

"If I ever get away," muttered Dirby, "I'm going back to Thrope. I'll work my father's loquat orchard and never again look at the sky.''

"Perhaps I'll join you there," said Hetzel. "Especially if you find yourself unable to pay my fee.''

"I'll pay you off in loquats if necessary." Dirby's eyes gleamed with malicious humor, which Hetzel found at least preferable to sulkiness and self-pity.

"Tomorrow I fly out into the back country," said Hetzel. "I'll be gone a day or two; you'll have to fend for yourself until I get back.''

"Be as mysterious as you like," Dirby grumbled, once more his usual self. "I'm in no position to complain.''

CHAPTER 9

Hetzel arrived at the transport depot early in the morning, to find that Janika had already arranged the rental of an air car. "It's an old Ray Standard, and it's supposed to be dependable."

"There's nothing a bit faster? We have considerable ground to cover."

"There's a new Hemus Cloudhopper, but it's more expensive."

"Money means nothing," said Hetzel. "Let's take the Hemus."

"They want to be paid in advance in case we kill ourselves: twenty SLU for two days, which includes insurance and energy."

Hetzel paid the account. They climbed into the air car. Hetzel checked out the controls and energy level, then took the vehicle aloft. "Did Vv. Byrrhis make any difficulty about letting you off?"

"Nothing to speak of. I told him that I wanted to take a friend out to Black Cliff Inn, and that was that."

Axistil and its environs became a set of unlikely patterns on the heave and fall of the downs. Hetzel brought a map to the navigation screen and established a course due north. "I want to investigate the Great Kykh-Kych Swamp," said Hetzel in response to Janika's questioning glance. "I don't know what I'll find—in fact, I don't know what I'm looking for. But if I don't go, I'll never know."

"You are a mysterious man, and mysteries are exasperating," said Janika. "I myself have no secrets whatever."

Hetzel wondered how much credence could be placed in this remark. Today she wore a short-sleeved blouse of soft-gray cloth trimmed with black piping, black trousers, and jaunty ankle boots—a costume that made the most of her supple figure. She wore no ornaments except a black ribbon binding her hair. An exceedingly attractive young woman, thought Hetzel, fresh and clean-looking, with an air of simplicity that was both charming and suspect.

"Why are you looking at me so intently?" she asked. "Is my nose red?"

"I marvel at your confidence. After all, I'm a stranger to you, and out here beyond the Reach, a stranger is usually a depraved murderer, or a sadistic fiend, or worse."

Janika laughed, perhaps a trifle uneasily. "Inside or outside the Reach—what's the difference?"

"You don't have too much to fear," said Hetzel. "I'm far too gallant for my own good, although only an Olefract could fail to notice that you are extremely pretty. You make a stimulating companion for a trip like this one."

"What kind of a trip is a trip like this one?"

"We intend to prove the innocence of one of your former lovers, and save him from the Exhibitory."

"You astonish me! My 'former lovers' are all far away, living the most torpid lives imaginable. I wonder which of them you refer to, and how he managed to get into such mischief."

"This one is a certain Gidion Dirby."

Janika frowned. "Gidion Dirby?"

"Yes. A blond young man, obstinate, wrongheaded, seething with emotion. So he is now. Three months ago he might have been a different person entirely."

"I remember Gidion Dirby, but our acquaintance was
. . . well almost casual. Certainly so, from my point of
view."

Hetzel looked down across the landscape—a savanna
carpeted with green-black furze and clots of spike trees.
In the far-eastern distance a glimmer of sea was visible,
then a blur of atmospheric murk. Hetzel asked, "How
did you happen to meet Gidion Dirby?"

"First," said Janika, "tell me what he's done, and also
why you're so mysterious."

"Gidion Dirby is suspected of assassinating two
Triarchs. I am not so much mysterious as confused and
suspicious."

"Confused about what? And who are you suspicious
of? Me? I haven't done anything."

"I'm confused about Istagam . . . and why there is so
much secrecy involved. Presumably the reason is money.
I'm suspicious because effectuators are paid to be suspicious, and I'm an effectuator. A high-class and expensive effectuator, needless to say. I'm suspicious of
you because you were associated with Gidion Dirby on
Tamar, and here you are on Maz."

"Sheer coincidence," said Janika.

"Possibly. Why were you on Tamar?"

"Tamar was where my money took me when I left
Varsilla. I worked for a week in the Central Market at
Twisselbane, and I worked another week in what they
call their Pageant of the Foam, because it paid quite
well. I had to dance and pose with not too many clothes
on—occasionally none at all. While we were rehearsing,
I met Gidion Dirby, who told me he was a spaceman,
and lonely."

"Like all spacemen."

"I saw him a few times, and he became . . . well . . .
possessive. Apparently he had fallen in love with me,
and I was having trouble enough with one of the directors of the pageant. So I stopped seeing Gidion Dirby. I

worked a week at the pageant, and some friends introduced me to Vv. Byrrhis, who mentioned that the Maz
Tourist Agency needed a receptionist. I was only too
pleased to leave the pageant and Director Swince. Vv.
Byrrhis made me sign a six-month contract and gave me
a ticket to Maz, and here I am."

"You never saw Gidion Dirby again?"

"I'd almost forgotten him until just now."

"Very odd." They flew over an arm of the sea, a
leaden expanse glistening with green luster. "You've
been here how long?"

"About three months."

"With another three months to go on your contract.
Then what?"

"I'm not sure. I'll have enough money to go almost
anywhere. I'd like to visit Earth."

"You might be disappointed. Earth is a most subtle
world. Very few outworlders feel at ease on Old Earth,
unless they have friends there."

Janika turned him an arch side glance. "Will you be
there?"

"I couldn't tell you where I'll be a week from now."

"Don't you ever want to settle down somewhere?"

"I've thought about it. Gidion Dirby has invited me
to his father's loquat orchard."

Janika made a sound of scornful amusement. "Gidion
Dirby. You came to Maz on his account?"

"No. I came to learn something about Istagam. But
the two matters might be connected."

Janika said, "Perhaps I'll become an effectuator. It
seems like fun. One always stays in the best hotels and
meets interesting people like myself, and there's always
a Sir Ivon Hacaway to pay the bills."

"It's not always like this."

"And what takes us out toward the Great Kykh-Kych
Swamp? Gidion Dirby business or Istagam?"

"Both. And then there's another most peculiar element to the case, by the name of Casimir Wuldfache."

The name seemed to mean nothing to Janika. For a period they rode in silence over a sprawling range of ancient basalt mountains, black crags protruding like rotten stumps from maroon detritus. Janika pointed. "Look yonder—the castle of the Viszt." She took up binoculars. "Warriors are returning from a campaign, probably against the Shimrod, and the tourists have been cheated again." She passed the binoculars to Hetzel and showed him where to look.

White skull faces bobbed and blinked under crested helmets of cast iron; aprons of black leather swung to the motion of the legs. To the rear rolled six wagons pulled by ten-legged reptiles, loaded with objects Hetzel could not identify.

"The Viszts are flyers," said Janika. "The wagons carry their wings. They climb the mountains, put on their wings, and glide on the updrafts. Then, when they locate their enemies—I can't think of a better word— they swoop down and attack."

"Curious creatures."

"You know how they breed, or mate?"

"Sir Estevan gave me a pamphlet. In fact, you did too. I know that they are ambisexual, and that they go out to war in order to breed."

"It seems a dreary life," Janika reflected. "They kill for love, and they die for love—all in a frenzy."

"They probably consider our love life rather dull," said Hetzel.

"My love life *is* rather dull," said Janika. "Vv. Swince, Gidion Dirby, Vv. Byrrhis."

"Have patience. Somewhere among the twenty-eight trillion folk of the Gaean Reach is Vv. Right."

"Half of them are women, luckily. That cuts down the search by half." Janika took up the binoculars. "I might as well take a look out over the swamp right now. There might be some kind of a fugitive or a divorce out there."

"What do you see?" asked Hetzel.

"Nothing. Not even a Gomaz, whom I wouldn't consider anyway."

They flew above a land of rolling moors with tarns of dark water in the hollows. Ahead, the course of the Dz River lay in languid curves and loops; beyond spread the Great Kykh-Kych Swamp. Hetzel examined the chart with attention.

Janika asked, "What are you looking for?"

"An island five miles or so from the north shore, where Gidion Dirby was marooned by a man named Banghart. Have you ever heard that name, incidentally?"

"Not to my knowledge."

"Three islands are possible. This one to the east"—Hetzel indicated the chart—"This one in the center, and this to the west. The center island is closest to the black circle on the chart."

"That's the castle of the old Kanitze sept, which was wiped out by the Ubaikh two hundred years ago, and Kykh-Kych Inn, which is now closed down."

"We're coming in over the east island. Look for a path leading to the mainland."

Hetzel circled the island—a hummock of twenty acres, crowned with a copse of iron trees and the tall rattling canes known as "galangal." There was no area suitable for discharge of cargo; no path led away to the mainland.

The central island lay twenty miles north—an area somewhat larger, with a level meadow marked and scarred as if by the arrival and departure of vehicles.

Hetzel hovered over the meadow. "This is the place." He pointed. "That iron tree yonder—there Dirby passed the night. . . . And there—the path leading to the shore! Here we pick up the thread of Dirby's adventures. Shall we land?"

"We're not supposed to land except in authorized locations," said Janika. "That's the rule, but it's not always obeyed."

Hetzel glanced at his watch. "We don't have all that much time if we want to meet the Ubaikh at the transport depot. So, we'd better fly on."

Janika looked at him in astonishment. "We're to meet whom?"

"The Ubaikh who witnessed the assassinations. If we want to learn the identity of the killer, he's the obvious person to ask."

"Suppose he says it was Gidion Dirby?"

"I don't think he will. But I intend to ask him, no matter what he says."

"You seem very zealous all of a sudden."

"Yes, the mood strikes me once in a while."

Janika looked down at the swamp, now only a few hundred feet below: an expanse of black slime; various tufts of reeds, lung-plant, white whisker; wandering rivulets of dark water. The path slanted this way and that, following a series of slanted quartzite outcrops. "If I knew what you were looking for, I could look too."

Hetzel pointed to the dun-colored loom of mainland ahead. "Look for a stone wall. Gidion Dirby found a stone wall and a gate and Sir Estevan Tristo waiting for him. Except it probably wasn't Sir Estevan. More likely Casimir Wuldfache."

Janika looked through the binoculars. "I see the wall and the gate. I don't see either Sir Estevan or Casimir Wolf-face, whatever his name is. Now I can see the old Kanitze castle."

"This is where Gidion Dirby passed several memorable months, or so I suspect. He described some of his adventures to me. His chair ejected him to the floor. Sir Estevan emptied a chamber pot over his head. He observed you dancing upon the surface of his brain without any clothes on."

"One thing you can take as certain," said Janika. "I

have never danced upon Gidion Dirby's brain."

"No question about this. You were evidently filmed at the Pageant of Foam on Tamar and the sequences adapted to the circumstances here. Almost certainly, Casimir Wuldfache turned the pot over Dirby's head, since Sir Estevan denies doing so. All in all a curious set of experiences."

"Unless Dirby is a madman, as I once suspected."

They approached the cyclopean bulk of the ruined Kanitze castle. The roof across the vast central keep had long since rotted away; the seven peripheral towers had tumbled to broken stubs surrounded by detritus. The tower at the far western edge of the complex had been fitted with a new roof and structurally refurbished— evidently the disused tourist inn.

Hetzel allowed the air car to drift quietly above the castle while he looked down through binoculars. He stared so long and so intently that Janika at last inquired, "What do you see?"

"Nothing very definite," said Hetzel. He put the binoculars in the rack and looked down at the ruined castle. In the shadows of the central keep he had observed a stack of crates, protected from the weather by a shroud of transparent membrane. Up from the castle rose a fume of danger, quivering like hot air.

"I don't dare to land," Hetzel muttered. "In fact, I feel the urgent desire to leave, before someone or something destroys us." He jerked the air car into motion; they skidded away to the west.

Janika looked back at the receding ruins. "This isn't quite the placid excursion I had expected."

"Perhaps I shouldn't have brought you."

"I'm not complaining. . . . So long as I escape with my life."

The castle of the extinct Kanitze became a dark smudge and disappeared into the murk.

"The rest of the trip should be relatively uneventful. The Ubaikh depot is safe ground, or so I'm told."

"The Olefract or the Liss patrol might think you're trying to sell weapons, and kill you."

"I've got Sir Estevan's translator. If necessary, I can explain."

"Not to the Liss. They believe what they see, and they're most suspicious."

"Well . . . they probably won't see us."

"I hope not."

The depot stood on a pebbly plain beside a white-and-orange target a hundred yards in diameter. Mountain shadows loomed above the north horizon; to west and east the plain extended into the blur of the sky. To the south, two miles from the depot, stood the castle of the Ubaikh sept—like the Kanitze ruins, a bulk of awesome proportions. Parapets surrounded the central keep; an inner tower rose another hundred feet to a squat roof of sullen maroon tiles. Seven barbicans, taller and more slender than those of the Kanitze ruins, guarded the keep, each joined to the parapets by an arched buttress. The area under the castle flickered with motion— Gomaz, and Gomaz bantlings at their routines and drills. Wagons rolled along an east road and a west road, loaded with what Hetzel took to be provender. There seemed to be flapping black forms in the air surrounding the towers. Down, down the figures drifted, darting, wheeling, diving, and swooping, occasionally, by dint of furious effort, gaining altitude before once more gliding.

Hetzel dropped the air car to the ground beside the depot. "We've got something less than an hour to wait, if the carrier is on schedule."

Half an hour passed. Across the sky came the carrier —an ellipsoidal compartment supported on four pulsor pods. It dropped to a landing at the exact center of the orange-and-white target. The entry port slid open; steps unfolded; a single figure disembarked. The carrier paused a moment, like a resting insect, then swept off at a slant to the south. Hetzel meanwhile had approached the Ubaikh with the language translator.

The Ubaikh paused to assess the situation, wattles distended but uncolored. He wore an iron collar, which appeared to indicate status, and carried a sword of pounded iron in a harness over his back. Hetzel halted ten feet from the Ubaikh—as close as he dared approach.

The Ubaikh's wattles remained a pallid white, with a network of pulsing green veins, indicating simple antagonism.

Hetzel spoke into the translator. "You have just now returned from Axistil." The instrument produced a set of hisses and squeaks, fluting up into inaudibility and down again.

The Ubaikh stood rigid, the white bone of his face immobile, the eyes glowing like black gems. Hetzel wondered whether it might be taking telepathic counsel with its fellows in the castle.

The Ubaikh hissed, clicked, squeaked; the translator printed out on the tape: "I have visited Axistil."

"What did you do there?"

"I yield no information."

Hetzel grimaced in frustration. "I have come far to talk to you, a noble and notable Ubaikh warrior."

The translator evidently failed to reproduce the exact implications of Hetzel's remark, for the Ubaikh emitted a hiss which the tape merely identified in red italics as "anger." The Ubaikh said, "My rank is high, and more than high: I am a chieftain. Did you come to traduce me in the very shadow of my castle?"

"Not at all," said Hetzel hastily. "There has been a misunderstanding. I came respectfully to request information of you."

"I yield no information."

"I will express my appreciation with a metal tool."

"Your bargains are worthless, like all Gaean bargains." Words appeared on the tape faster than Hetzel could read them. "The Gomaz were defeated by metal and energy, not by courage. It indicates weakness that the Gaeans and Olefract and Liss hide in metal cells and send forth mechanical objects to fight for them. The Gomaz are strong warriors, the Ubaikh are supreme. They often defeat the Kzyk, whom the Gaeans choose to favor. The Gaeans are deceitful. The Ubaikh demand equal access to the secrets of metal and energy. Since we are denied, the Kzyk must suffer a Class III 'Rivalry' war, to the detriment of our long ages of love and war and esteem. The Liss and the Olefract are intractable cowards. The Gaeans are cowards, traitors and lie mongers. The Kzyk will never profit from the scandal of their activities. Bantlings and striplings must be tested and trained. The Kzyk will become a race of diseased monsters, sapped of strength, unworthy of love, but the Ubaikh will destroy the sept. We too are anxious for the secrets of metal and energy, but we will never become suppliants."

The spate of words ended abruptly. Hetzel made what he thought might be a concilliatory statement: "The Triarchy intends justice for the noble Ubaikh sept."

The Ubaikh's wattles become mottled with green patches. Hetzel watched in fascination. The Ubaikh produced sounds, and the translator printed out a new storm of words. "The remark is empty of meaning. The Gomaz are constrained by strength of metal and bite of energy. Otherwise we would bring a Class III war upon our enemies. The Triarchy is a monument to pusillanimity. Will the Triarchs dare to fight any of us? They sit in fear."

"The Triarchs were killed before they could deal with your business. Two of your companions were killed as well."

The Ubaikh stood silently.

Hetzel said, "The killer of these individuals has wronged us all. Will you return to Axistil and help to apprehend the criminal?"

"I will never return to Axistil. The Triarchs are excellently killed. The Gomaz are an oppressed folk; their current status is a tragedy. Let the Gaeans teach all Gomaz the secrets of fire and metal, rather than just the Kzyk, then all will join to defeat the mutual enemy. Be off with you; this is the vicinity of the superlative Ubaikh sept. I would grind you to a powder if I did not fear your weapons." The creature turned and stalked away.

The Gomaz were an obstinate race, thought Hetzel. He returned to the air car.

Janika asked, "Well, who killed the Triarchs?"

"He wouldn't tell me anything except that he approved of the whole affair." Hetzel took the air car aloft.

"Now where?"

"Where are the Kzyk territories?"

"A hundred miles north, more or less. Beyond the Shimkish Mountains yonder."

Hetzel studied the chart, then considered the sun, which hung halfway down the western sky. He turned the car toward the Black Cliff Inn, and Janika relaxed into her seat.

"What do you want with the Kzyk?"

Hetzel passed her the translator tape. "It's more or less a trade on the sins of the Gaeans."

Janika read the tape. "It sounds as if he went to Axistil to protest favors to the Kzyk."

"And why should the Kzyk get special treatment?"

"I don't know," said Janika.

"I don't know either. But it might be Istagam."

CHAPTER 10

The Black Cliff Inn hung half over the brink of a mighty basalt scarp, under a complex of titanic ruins. Below spread a landscape that might have been contrived by a mad poet: a sodden moor clotted with turf of an unreal magenta, clumped with black water willow and an occasional eruption of extravagantly tall and frail galangal reeds glistening like silver threads.

Hetzel came out upon the terrace, to find a dozen other guests taking refreshment and enjoying the smoky-green sunset. He seated himself at a table and ordered a beaker of pomegranate punch with two stone-and-silver goblets. The perquisites of his occupation were occasionally most pleasant, thought Hetzel. The air drifting up from the plain brought a musky reek of moss and galangal and a dozen unnamable balsams. From far across the moor, thin, high-pitched calls shivered the quiet, and once a distant ululation evoked so much mystery and solitude that the hair rose at the back of Hetzel's neck.

Janika slipped into the chair beside him. She wore a soft white frock and had combed her hair into lustrous loose curls. A most appealing creature, thought Hetzel, and quite probably as careless and candid as she appeared. He poured her a goblet of punch. "Sunset at the Black Cliff Inn is a remarkable occasion, and Vv. Byrrhis is a remarkable man for having created all this."

"No doubt about that," said Janika in an even voice. "Vv. Byrrhis is a remarkable man."

"These inns—how many are there? Six? Seven? . . . They represent considerable capital. I wonder how Byrrhis financed such an operation."

Janika gave her fingers a flick to indicate her lack of interest in the matter. "I'm not supposed to know anything about it—and actually, I don't. But. . . it's well known that Sir Estevan Tristo is very wealthy."

"It seems a chancy investment," said Hetzel. "There's no possibility of firm title to the real estate."

"Vv. Byrrhis has as good title as anyone else. The Gomaz don't object; ruined castles are taboo. Black Cliff is famous for sunsets," said Janika. "And tonight we'll see ghosts."

"Ghosts? Are you serious?"

"Of course. The Gomaz call the plain yonder the Place of Wandering Dreams."

"Do persons other than the Gomaz see the ghosts?"

"Certainly. A few dull souls see only wisps of marsh gas, or white-veiled night crakes, but no one believes such drab nonsense."

Other guests came out on the terrace. "The inn must be almost full," said Hetzel. "I suspect that Vv. Byrrhis is coining money."

"I don't know. He seems harried and anxious most of the time. I suspect that he isn't as prosperous as he would like to be, but who is?"

"Certainly not I."

"Suppose you solved this case brilliantly and Gidion Dirby gave you a million-SLU bonus—what would you do with it?"

"More likely a million loquats from Gidion Dirby. From Sir Ivon Hacaway . . ." Hetzel gave his head a rueful shake. "First I have to solve the case." He brought forth the translator tape and studied it a moment. "The tirade include a few scintillas of information, no doubt by mistake. Someone is teaching the

Kzyk 'secrets of fire and metal.' Who? Why? Istagam naturally comes to mind. The Kzyk provide labor and are paid off in technology, which I presume to be illegal. The Ubaikh object. The Liss and the Olefract are also certain to object, so their Triarchs are killed off for this reason. Just speculation, of course."

"A rather frightening speculation." Janika looked uneasily up and down the terrace.

Hetzel put away the tape. "Tomorrow we'll visit the Kzyk, or at least look them over. But now let's talk of something more interesting. Lljiano Reyes of Varsilla, for instance."

"I don't want to talk about me. . . . Though, for a fact . . . well, I'd better not say it."

"You've aroused my curiosity."

"It's not all that interesting. When I wanted to leave Palestria, everyone said I was foolish and perverse, which may be true. But tonight at the Black Cliff Inn is what I wanted to find." She made an exasperated gesture. "I know I'm not making myself clear. But look, up there hangs the green moon, and here we sit looking out over the Place of Wandering Dreams, waiting for ghosts and drinking pomegranate punch, no ghosts."

Hetzel had no comment to make; for a period they sat in silence.

Across the moon floated a gaunt black shape on slow-beating wings. "There's a ghost now," said Hetzel.

"I don't think so. Ghosts don't fly like that. . . . It's too long and frail for a gargoyle. . . . It's probably a black angel."

"And what's a black angel?"

"If I'm right, it's the thing we just saw."

Hetzel rose to his feet. "Hunger is confusing both of us. I suggest that we have our dinner."

Within the ruins of the central tower, six iron legs supported a stone disk forty feet in diameter—the adjunct to some ancient Gomaz rite. At the center a post of twisted black iron rose twelve feet, to fracture into several black iron branches tipped with small clusters of yellow flames—luminous fruits on a grotesque tree. Hetzel and Janika mounted iron steps; a steward in green-and-black livery conducted them to a table spread with white linen, laid with silver and crystal.

Hetzel looked up to see open sky, with wan moonlight slanting in against the northern wall. "And in bad weather, what then?"

"In the rainy season we send people south to the Andantinai Desert, where they can see volcanoes and carrier kites and the Great Cairn. Vv. Byrrhis has thought of everything."

"Vv. Byrrhis is a very resourceful man, and no doubt very stimulating to work with."

Janika laughed. "He wanted to take me out to Golgath Inn on the Plain of Skulls, but I thought better of it, and he hasn't been stimulating since. If he knew I were here with you, he'd be furious. Or so I suppose. Even on so innocent an occasion."

Vv. Byrrhis' emotional problems seemed remote and inconsequential. "Whom does he think you're here with?"

"He didn't ask. I didn't specify."

The steward served a salad of native herbs, which Hetzel found pleasantly tart; a ragout of ingredients beyond conjecture; thin cakes of crisp bread; two flasks of imported Zenc wine, the first yellow, the second dark amber swimming with an oily violet luster.

Janika performed the conventional Zenc wine ceremony, pouring half a goblet of dark, wiping away the luster with a square of soft fabric, and immediately filling the goblet with yellow.

"Except for the wine, everything is Maz produce," Janika said. "When I first arrived, I thought everything tasted of moss and hardly ate anything; now I'm much more tolerant. But I still think of Varsilla sea bakes and pepper pots and yams stuffed with mulberries . . . Let's take our dessert out on the terrace and look for ghosts."

The dessert, a pale-green sherbet, was served with goblets of a pungent hot brew steeped from the bark of a desert shrub. For an hour they stood on the terrace over the plain. They heard far wistful calls and soft secret hooting, but saw no ghosts. Janika presently went off to bed. Hetzel drank another cup of tea, and once more considered the translator tape.

A most complicated situation, he reflected, with the parts not merely contradictory but apparently unrelated. High stakes were obviously involved; no one would go to such lengths to motivate Gidion Dirby for trivial reasons. And how strange that Casimir Wuldfache, whom he had traced to Twisselbane on Tamar for Madame X, should now play a role in the Dirby-Istagam affair. Coincidence? Hetzel gave his head a dubious shake. The unmistakable reek of danger hung in the air; persons who had evolved such elaborate schemes would hardly balk at a life or two; perhaps they had already killed a Liss, an Olefract, and two Ubaikh Gomaz. Double vigilance was necessary; he must guard Janika as well as himself.

During the night Hetzel was aroused by the muted whine of an energy converter. He went to the window and looked out through the night. Across the sky, dim in the light of the low green moon, drifted the shape of a receding air car. Odd, thought Hetzel. Odd indeed.

In the pale light of morning, Hetzel and Janika breakfasted on the terrace. Janika seemed wan and thoughtful, and Hetzel wondered at her somber face. He asked, "Did you sleep well?"

"Well enough."

"You seem very pensive this morning."

"I don't want to go back to Dogtown and the tourist agency."

"We've got to go back to Dogtown," said Hetzel. "But you don't have to go back to the tourist agency."

"I signed a six-month contract. I'd lose half of what

I've got coming if I quit now."

Hetzel sipped his tea. "Since you don't like Dogtown, where do you want to go?"

"I don't know."

"Varsilla?"

"Oh . . . sooner or later. But not just now. I don't know what I want to do. I guess I'm just in a bad mood."

Hetzel thought a few moments. "Vv. Byrrhis might let you break the contract."

"I don't think so. He's made jocular remarks that weren't really funny. But maybe I'll quit anyway."

"Vv. Byrrhis might be more cooperative than you expect. He'd get no benefit from a sulky or apathetic receptionist. In the second place . . . But why anticipate events?"

Janika took Hetzel's hand and squeezed it. "I feel more cheerful already."

Hetzel settled the account. Janika made a tentative effort to pay half the bill, which Hetzel refused to allow, citing the generosity of his client, Sir Ivon Hacaway. They went out to the landing stage and climbed into the Hemus Cloudhopper. "Good-bye, Black Cliff Inn," said Hetzel. He looked at Janika. "Why the long face?"

"I don't like to say good-bye to anything."

"You're as sentimental as Gidion Dirby," said Hetzel. He took the air car aloft. "Now to Axistil by way of Kzyk castle. If we're lucky, we'll catch a glimpse of Istagam."

Janika showed no enthusiasm for the detour. "There won't be much to see from the air, and it's worth our lives to land."

"We won't take chances, especially since a visit to the Triskelion will probably clear things up."

"Oh? What will you find there?"

"The agenda, or the calendar, whatever it's called, of the Triarchs. I want to learn how long ago the Ubaikh scheduled their visit."

"That doesn't seem too important."

"There you're wrong. It's the critical element in the entire case, or so I believe." Hetzel examined the chart. "We fly north across the Ubaikh domain, over the Shimkish Mountains, and down across this . . . what is it called? The Steppe of Long Bones?"

"Because of a great battle a thousand years ago. The Ubaikh, the Kzyk, and the Aqzh fought the Hissau. It was a 'Hate' war, because the Hissau are nomads and pariahs who waylay bantlings of other septs while they're trying to reach their home castles after being born. . . . If burrowing out of a corpse could be called 'birth.' "

"How do the bantlings find their way home?"

"Telepathy. Only about a third survive the trip."

"It seems a harsh system," Hetzel reflected. "And the Gomaz would seem cruel and harsh, at least in human terms."

"Because we're not fused telepathically into a single entity."

"Exactly. They probably consider us strange and cruel too, for reasons equally irrational. . . . There's the Ubaikh castle, over to the west."

Janika looked through the binoculars. "Troops are leaving the castle. They're marching off somewhere— perhaps against the Kzyks. Or the Kaikash, or the Aqzh."

The Ubaikh castle disappeared astern; ahead loomed the Shimkish Mountains—black shards above a tumble of pale-green and brown velvet. Beyond lay a plain of featureless gray-blue murk—the Steppe of Long Bones, which slowly expanded to fill half the horizon. . . . A sound from the engines attracted Hetzel's attention. The pulsors had become audible, whirring at the highest level of audibility, then gradually signing down the scale. Hetzel stared in consternation at the energy gauge.

Janika noticed his expression. "What's the trouble?"

"No more energy. The batteries are dead."

"But the gauge shows half a charge!"

"Either it's broken or somebody disconnected the conduit and then killed the batteries. In either case, we're going down."

"But we're miles from anywhere!"

"We've got the radio." Hetzel manipulated the dial. "We don't seem to have a radio, after all."

"But what could have happened? These cars are supposed to be carefully serviced!"

Hetzel recalled the air car he had glimpsed the night before. "Someone has decided that we've lived long enough. He left us just enough charge to get well away from the inn."

The air car floated down upon the wind-scoured pebbles of the Steppe of Long Bones. The two sat in silence. Hetzel studied the chart. "We're about here. Ubaikh castle is forty miles across the mountains. Kzyk castle is sixty miles northwest. Our best chance would seem to be the Ubaikh transport station on the other side of the mountains. The mountains are harder, but we should find water. There's no water on the steppe."

Janika chewed her lip. "The radio can't be fixed?"

Hetzel removed the case. One glance at the broken plates was enough. "The radio is done. If you like, you can stay with the car while I go for help. It might be easier for you."

"I'd rather come with you."

"I'd rather you did too." Hetzel scowled down at the chart. "If we had flown south from Black Cliff Inn, back toward Axistil, we'd have come down in the middle of the Kykh-Kych Swamp, with no chance whatever."

"We don't have much chance out here."

"Forty miles isn't all that bad—two or three days' hike, depending upon the terrain. What kind of wild beasts might we find?"

Janika looked around the sky. "Gargoyles live in the mountains. They prey on baby Gomaz, but if they're hungry, they'll attack anything. At night the lalu come out. Last night you could hear them out on the plain. And we might see ixxen—the white foxes of Maz. They're blind, but they run in packs of two or three hundred. They're dreadful creatures; they capture baby Gomaz and raise them to be ixxen, so sometimes you'll look out on the plain and see naked Gomaz running on all fours, and they're the eyes for the pack until the pack decides to tear them apart. If we meet any Gomaz, they could consider us field prey and kill us"

Hetzel rummaged through the various storage compartments in hopes of locating a spare power cell, but vainly; he found nothing. Descending to the ground, he searched the horizons. Solitude everywhere. He checked the charts once more, then pointed toward the mountains. "There's a pass directly under that double-pronged peak. From there we should see a ridge that runs a few miles south of the Ubaikh castle. We won't get lost. With luck we'll make forty miles in two days, provided we're not killed; I'm carrying two pistols, a knife and ten grenades. We've got a good chance for survival. I'll bring the translator in case we encounter any stray Gomaz. Since there's no point in delay, we might as well get started. If you've got spare boots, you'd better bring them. Also your cloak."

"I'm ready."

They set out to the south, across a spongy turf of black lichen. Puffs of dark dust rose behind them; their footprints were clearly defined.

"Ixxen will follow if they come on the tracks. It's said that they sense the warmth even after days."

Hetzel took her hand; her fingers closed on his. "I'm certain that we'll reach Axistil safely, and you can be sure that the folk on Varsilla would marvel to see you now—tramping across the Steppe of Long Bones in company with a vagabond like myself."

"I don't think I'm fated to die just yet. . . . Who would do such a thing to us?"

"Can't you guess?"

"No. Gidion Dirby? Unlikely. The Ubaikh? He would never think of such an exploit, and he knows nothing of air cars."

"What of Vv. Byrrhis?"

Janika's mouth fell open. "Why should he bear us malice? Because of me?"

"Perhaps."

"I can't believe it. And never forget, the air car belongs to the tourist agency, which is to say, Vv. Byrrhis, and he loves his SLU."

"In due course all will be made known. Meanwhile, if you see anything edible, by all means point it out."

"I'm hardly an authority on such things. I've heard that just about everything is poisonous."

"We can travel two days, or three or four, if necessary, without food."

Janika said nothing. They walked on in silence. Hetzel reflected that all his residual oddments of suspicion in regard to the girl might be dismissed; she would hardly subject herself to hardship of such magnitude. On the other hand, if she were the accomplice of Vv. Byrrhis, he might well elect to rid himself of her as well as Hetzel.

The sun rose toward the zenith; by insensible degrees the Shimkish peaks and ridges came to dominate the sky. Meanwhile, terrain grew ever more difficult: from pebbles and sand and fields of black lichen, to low slopes grown with prickle bush and black waxweed, and the outlying spurs of the foothills.

Three hours of climbing brought them to the crest of a ridge, where they rested and looked back the way they had come. Janika leaned against Hetzel; he put his arm around her. "Are you tired?"

"It's something I've decided not to think about."

"Very sensible. We've come a good distance." He looked through the binoculars northward over the steppe. "I can't see the air car anymore."

Janika pointed off across the distance. "Look over there. Something is moving; I can't make out what it is."

"Gomaz—marching in a column with four wagons. They're heading in our general direction, but to the west."

"They'd be Kzyks," said Janika. "Out patrolling, or maybe off to raid the Ubaikh, or one of the septs west of the Ubaikh; I forget what they call themselves. How many do you see?"

"Too many to count. Several hundred, at a guess. . . . We'd better get moving."

For a period the way was easy, up the ridge, then across a narrow plateau. Beyond rose the main bulk of the Shimkish Mountains, with the landmark crag prominent.

At a freshet of water they drank, then continued to climb, now resting frequently.

"It'll be easier coming down the other side," said Hetzel, "and a lot faster."

"If we ever reach the top. I'm starting to worry about the next ten steps."

"We'd better go on before our muscles stiffen. Like you, I'm not accustomed to this mountain climbing."

The sun moved around the sky. Two hours before sunset, Hetzel and Janika toiled up from a vine-choked ravine and out on an upland meadow, watered by a small stream. Gasping, sweating, smarting from scratches, stings, and bites, they sank down upon a flat rock. A sward of small heart-shaped leaves carpeted the meadow. A hundred yards east stood a forest of growths that for the most part Hetzel could not name: a few bloodwoods, with trunks dark red, and clotted black foliage; purple tree ferns; clumps of giant galangal reeds. A quartermile west stood an even denser forest of bloodwoods. Certain areas of the meadow had been trampled, and an odd reek hung in the air—an odor musky and foul, which Hetzel associated with organic decay, although nothing dead was immediately visible.

From time to time on their way up the mountainside

they had glimpsed wild creatures: bounding black weasels, all eyes, hair and fangs; a long, low creature like a headless armadillo, creeping on a hundred short legs; white grasshopperlike rodents, with heads uncomfortably similar to the crested white skulls of the Gomaz. A torpid reptile twenty feet long had watched them pass with an uncanny semblance of intelligence. In the ravine they had disturbed a shoal of flying snakes—pale, fragile creatures sliding through the air on long lateral frills. They had seen neither ixxen nor bantlings, and nothing but thorns and insects had caused them discomfort. Hetzel now noticed a dozen square-winged shapes wheeling through the air, with heads drooping on long muscular necks—gargoyles. They had glided down from a high crag, to swoop and circle a hundred feet above the eastward forest. Most unpleasant creatures, thought Hetzel. Their flight, so he noted, seemed to be bringing them closer to the meadow.

Hetzel now became aware of a strange strident sound, shrilling up and down, in and out of audibility, to a complex cadence that Hetzel could not quite grasp. He knew at once what the sound portended.

"Gomaz!" whispered Janika. "They're coming toward us!"

Hetzel leaped to his feet; he looked this way and that for a covert. The ravine from which they had only just emerged would serve; more appealing was a tooth of rock a few yards north, a little crag of rotten basalt, luxuriantly grown over with iron plant. He took Janika's hand; they scrambled up the crag and threw themselves flat on the crest under the massive black leaves.

At the same instant, the Gomaz emerged from the east forest—a column four abreast, marching to a skew-legged goose step. At the east bank of the stream the Gomaz halted; the ululating whine of their song diminished into inaudibility. They broke ranks and went to wade in the stream.

Janika whispered in Hetzel's ear, "They're Ubaikh—a war party."

Hetzel peered down at the Gomaz. "How do you know they're Ubaikh?"

"By the helmets. Look! See that one standing off to the side? Isn't he the one who just returned from Axistil?"

"I don't know. They all look alike to me."

"He's the same one. He's still wearing that iron collar and carrying a steel sword."

The Gomaz climbed from the water and reformed ranks, but made no move to proceed. Overhead soared the gargoyles, long necks bent low.

Hetzel pointed to the forest of bloodwoods at the western end of the meadow. "More gargoyles!"

A second band of Gomaz marched into view, singing their own wavering, whining polyphony, followed by a train of four wagons. "The Kzyk," Janika whispered. "The same band we saw this morning!"

The Kzyk marched forward as if the Ubaikh were invisible. At the edge of the stream they broke ranks, as the Ubaikh had done, and waded into the water. The Ubaikh stood rigid and motionless, and presently the Kzyk returned to the west bank of the stream and reformed ranks; they too stood stiff and stern.

Three minutes passed, during which, so far as Hetzel could see, neither Ubaikh nor Kzyk twitched a muscle. Then from the Kzyk ranks a warrior stepped forth. He paced up and down along the west bank of the stream with an odd strutting motion, raising high a leg, extending and placing it upon the ground with exaggerated delicacy.

From the Ubaikh ranks came a warrior, who strutted in similar fashion along the east bank of the stream.

Three more Kzyk came forth, to perform a set of bizarre postures, of a significance totally incomprehensible to Hetzel. Three Ubaikh performed in similar postures on the east bank. "It must be a kind of war dance," Hetzel whispered.

"War dance or love dance."

On each side of the stream, while the white sequin of sun sank down the darkening green sky and the wind sighed through the bloodwood trees, the Gomaz warriors strutted and postured, swayed, dipped and jerked. They began to sing—at first a whisper, then a fluting louder and more intense, then a throbbing wail, which sent chills up and down Hetzel's skin. Janika shuddered and closed her eyes and pressed close against Hetzel.

The song vibrated up and out of audibility, then stopped short. The silence creaked with tension. The striders and dancers wheeled quietly back to their ranks.

The engagement began. Warriors leaped the stream, their jaws clattering together, to confront an opponent. Each feinted, ducked, dodged, attempting to grip his adversary on the neck, with the mandibles now protruding from his jaw sockets.

Hetzel turned away his eyes; the spectacle was awful and wonderful; screams of passionate woe, wails of exaltation, tore at his brain. Janika lay shuddering; he put his arm around her and kissed her face, then drew away aghast; had he been swept away on a telepathic torrent? He lay stiff, clenching his mind against the tides of murderous erotic fervor.

Victors began to appear—those who had gripped their opponents' necks, either to cut a nerve or inject a hormone, for suddenly the defeated warrior became submissive, while the victor implanted its spawn into the victim's thorax, then ate the nubbin at the back of the limp creature's throat.

The battle ended; from the meadow came a new sound, half-moan, half-sigh. Of the original combatants, half remained alive. Originally there had been more Kzyk than Ubaikh, as was now the case, but the Kzyk showed no disposition to attack the survivors, who included—so Hetzel was pleased to see—the chieftain who had witnessed the assassinations at the Triskelion.

Overhead, the gargoyles circled, then one by one wheeled off and flapped away to the crags. "When the war is fought for hate," said Janika, "there are no survivors among the losers, and the gargoyles carry off the corpses. But the Ubaikh and the Kzyk will leave guards until the infants break out into the air." She looked at Hetzel in consternation. "What about us? How will we get away?"

"If necessary, I have my gun," said Hetzel. "We'll have to spend the night up here. There's probably no better place, in any event."

A moment or two went by. Janika looked sidewise toward Hetzel. "A little while ago you kissed me."

"So I did."

"Then you stopped."

"I was afraid that the Gomaz telepathy was getting to me. It didn't seem dignified. There's no telepathy now, of course." Hetzel kissed her again.

"I'm tired and dirty and miserable," said Janika. "I undoubtedly look awful."

"The formality in our relationship seems to be breaking down," said Hetzel. "What would they say in Varsilla if they could see you now?"

"I can't imagine. . . . I don't want to imagine. . . ."

CHAPTER 11

The night was long and dreary. Hetzel and Janika, wrapped in their cloaks, slept the sleep of exhaustion. At dawn they awoke cramped and sore and chilled. Hetzel peered out over the meadow. The Ubaikh huddled east of the stream; the Kzyk had formed a similar group to the west. With the coming of daylight, they brought forward their wagons and unloaded caldrons of food. The Ubaikh crossed the stream, and ate on even terms with the Kzyks, then returned to where they had passed the night. For a few minutes they wandered the meadow, examining the corpses of the previous evening's battle; then they began a colloquy, half telepathic, half through the medium of whistles and trills. The Ubaikh chieftain seemed to present a fervent exhortation. The Kzyks also deliberated together, then began to whistle derisively at the Ubaikh, who became stiff and haughty. The chieftain began strutting and stalking, but to a quicker pulse than on the evening previously. No longer did the warrior seem to preen; they moved curtly; their gestures were harsh and emphatic. The singing started—staccato phrases, shrill and domineering. Down from the crags came the gargoyles, to soar with drooping necks, peering intently at the events below.

The singing halted; the warriors formed ranks as before. Hetzel suddenly jerked to his feet.

"They'll see you!" said Janika.

"I can't let that Ubaikh get killed. He's the only dependable witness. Also, I like the look of those wagons. Come on down; hurry, before they start to fight."

They scrambled back down the back side of the crag. Hetzel stepped out upon the meadow. "Halt!" He spoke into the translator, with the volume at full. "The battle must cease. Break your ranks. Obey me, because I have weapons to kill all here and leave all corpses for the gargoyles." Hetzel raised his hand to the sky; one, two, three gargoyles exploded in gouts of purple flame and black smoke. A few charred fragments fell to the ground.

Hetzel pointed to the Ubaikh chieftain. "You must come with me. I will tolerate no more of your unrealistic arrogance. We will ride in the Kzyk wagons. They will take us to the Kzyk transport depot. Kzyk, prepare to march. Ubaikh, disperse; return to your castle. But both sides may leave guards to protect the bantlings." Hetzel turned and signaled to Janika. "Come."

The Gomaz had stood rigid as stone statues. Hetzel pointed to the chief. "You must come with me. Cross the stream and stand by the wagons."

The Ubaikh chieftain made a set of shrill, furious sounds, which the translator was unable to paraphrase. Hetzel took a step forward. "I am impatient. Ubaikh, disperse! Return to your castle! And you"—he pointed to the Ubaikh chieftain—"cross the stream!"

The air was full of resentful whistles. A Kzyk chieftain emitted an angry scream. The translator tape printed: "Who are you to give such orders?"

"I am a Gaean overlord! I have come to investigate the problems of the Gomaz. I need this Ubaikh chieftain as my witness; I cannot allow his death at this time."

"I would not have been killed," declared the chieftain.

"I intended to slaughter two dozen Kzyk and void upon their carcasses."

"You must postpone this exploit," said Hetzel. "To the wagons; smartly, now!"

The Ubaikh and the Kzyk stared at each other, indecisive and crestfallen. Hetzel said, "Who does not wish to obey me? Let him step forward!"

Neither Ubaikh nor Kzyk moved. Hetzel pointed his gun and destroyed two corpses—a Ubaikh and a Kzyk. A wail of awe and horror arose from the Gomaz. "To the wagons," said Hetzel.

The Ubaikh chieftain trudged ungraciously to the Kzyk wagons. The remaining Ubaikh moved across the meadow and stood in a restless group. The Kzyk, without hesitation, formed ranks and marched westward. Hetzel, Janika, and the Ubaikh chieftain climbed upon a wagon, which lurched off after the warriors. "This is somewhat better than walking," said Hetzel.

"I agree," said Janika.

The wagon rolled down from the heights, with the Ubaikh crouched in surly silence. Suddenly it hissed forth a set of emphatic polysyllables. Hetzel looked at the translator printout, which read: "Since alien creatures came to Maz, events go topsy-turvy. In the old days, conditions were better."

"Events still go well enough for the Gomaz," said Hetzel. "If they had not gone forth on a mission of conquest, they would not now be subject to control."

"Easy for you to say," was the response. "We conquer because this is our style of life. We do as we must."

"We defend ourselves for the same reason. You can be thankful that we have not destroyed the Gomaz race, as the Liss would prefer. The Gaeans are not callous murderers; hence, I ask your aid in fixing guilt upon the Triskelion assassin."

"It is a trivial matter."

"Who, then, was the assassin?"

"A Gaean."

"But which Gaean?"

"I do not know."

"Then how do you koow it's a Gaean?"

"I can show the fact, and then my duty to you is complete; no more need be said."

The Kzyk warriors uttered sudden screams of excitement. Hetzel stood up in the wagon, but saw only the Shimkish slopes and the stony gray steppe. The Kzyk goaded the draft worms; the wagons rumbled and bounded along the trail, the worms humping and collapsing; humping, collapsing; humping, collapsing.

Hetzel spoke a question into the translator. "Why the sudden excitement?"

"They have now discovered the Ubaikh plot."

"What plot?"

"Last night we feinted a raid in force over the Shimkish, to entice their most"—here the translator underlined the word "virile" in red—"away from the castle, while our greatest forces raided the traitors' castle. The Kzyk have now divined the plan. They hurry to defend their castle; this is a Class III war, to the extinction."

The worms became tired and slackened their pace; the Kzyk warriors loped ahead, kicking up puffs of dust behind their thrusting feet, and presently were lost to view among the moss hummocks, which here gave variety to the bleak landscape.

At noon the wagon stopped at an oasis, a pond of muddy water surrounded by a copse of rag trees and a few stunted galangals. A wind blew from the south, flogging the black rag shreds; the galangals snapped and clattered. Hetzel and Janika descended from the wagon and walked down to the pond. The surrounding mud showed hundreds of small spiked footprints, where ixxen had swarmed the previous evening.

Hetzel and Janika fastidiously skirted the pond, both thirsty but loath to drink, for the pond exhaled a sweet-foul odor. The Kzyk teamsters showed no restraint; they plunged into the water, wallowed, soaked and drank without compunction, and further soiled the water. They were joined by the Ubaikh chieftain. Hetzel looked at Janika. "How thirsty are you?"

"Not that thirsty."

"I guess I'm not either."

The wagons proceeded into the northeast. The Shimkish Mountains were gone; the steppe extended bare and featureless in all directions until it joined the sky.

Hetzel went to confer with the Kzyk teamster. "Where is the transport depot that serves the Kzyk?"

"It is near the castle."

"Take us to the transport depot."

"Your command is understood."

"Do you travel by night?"

"Naturally; but slowly. The worms will wish to rest."

"How long before we arrive?"

"Midmorning tomorrow. I fear that we shall miss the fighting."

"There will, no doubt, be another occasion."

"So I would presume."

Hetzel returned to Janika. "We spend tonight in the wagon. No doubt you're hungry."

"When I think of what there is to eat—not too hungry."

"When we return to Axistil, we will dine at the Beyranion, and order all the things you like the best."

"That will be nice."

Hetzel appraised the Ubaikh, speculating whether he might choose to attack during the darkness in the hope of possessing himself of Hetzel's weapons. From the human standpoint, this would seem a strong possibility, but such an act might be alien to the Gomaz psychology. In any event, wariness was certainly warranted.

Shortly before sunset, the wagon arrived at another water hole, and this time Hetzel and Janika abandoned all compunction and drank.

The sun sank; the sky displayed a few muted colors— lilac and apple green, a band of purple; then came the long dim dusk, then night. Hetzel drew his gun and held it pointed at the Ubaikh, who never so much as shifted his position. Janika dozed, then slept until moonrise, when she awoke with a jerk, perplexed to find herself in a wagon rolling across the Steppe of Long Bones. For an hour she kept watch while Hetzel slept, and when the wagons halted, he awoke. Something huge and manlike stood off in the moonlight, a being twenty feet high with a bony white head and carapace of a Gomaz. It uttered a chattering whinny, then lumbered off to the south. "An ogre!" whispered Janika. "I've heard about them; I never thought I'd see one. They're supposed to be ferocious."

The wagons continued once more. The great green moon lifted into the sky, making the steppe a place of eerie beauty. Hetzel dozed again; he awoke to find Janika asleep, her head in his lap, and the Ubaikh as before.

Nighttime waned; a streak of submarine light appeared in the east; the sun appeared, rising behind a range of distant hills.

The Kzyk set the worms into a more rapid motion; the wagons rumbled across the steppe and presently entered an area cultivated with pod plants and fruit bushes. The wagons turned upon a gravel road, which slanted up the hillside. At the crest, the Kzyk castle came into view—a magnificent quatrefoil keep surrounded by a ring of slender spires, joined to the keep by high walkways. The Ubaikh attack had already been launched; the areas to the south and west of the castle seethed with activity.

In the middle distance, four tall gantries rose indistinct in the murk. Hetzel was unable to divine their purpose. Siege machines? They seemed too frail, too tall, too top-heavy for any such use. Between the gantries and the castle, a mass of warriors eddied and swirled in movement too complex for any immediate comprehension.

At the foot of the slope stood the transport station, a structure identical to that beside the Ubaikh castle.

The wagons rolled down the hill, suddenly silent and easy on the heavy lichenlike turf. The Kzyk teamsters paid no heed to the Ubaikh army, nor did the Ubaikh chieftain; they exercised to the full that Gomaz attribute transliterated as *kxis'sh*—a lordly and contemptuous disregard for circumstances below one's dignity to notice.

Hetzel began to apprehend the evolutions of the army, as whole platoons performed the strutting display of ostentatious challenge and aggressive sexuality that Hetzel had observed on the Shimkish meadow. Every element of the army, in turn, so displayed itself, then returned to the rear. Meanwhile, the great wooden gantries moved closer to Kzyk castle, sliding on timber rollers.

The wagon halted by the transport station; Hetzel, Janika, and the Ubaikh chieftain alighted. The wagons proceeded toward the Kzyk castle, passing within fifty yards of the posturing Ubaikh warriors. Each party ignored the others.

The front of the depot displayed a placard printed in those red-and-black ideograms developed by men to communicate with the Gomaz. Janika puzzled out the significance of the marks. "We're in luck—I think. The carrier arrives at middle afternoon on alternate days, and unless I've miscalculated, today is the day. What time is it now?"

"Just about noon."

"I feel as if we've been gone months. I won't say that I've regretted this adventure, but I'll be glad to see civilization again. I'll enjoy a bath."

"I'll enjoy arriving alive," said Hetzel. "To the dismay of our enemies."

"Enemies?"

"There must be at least two, one of whom is almost certainly Vv. Byrrhis, or—as Gidion Dirby knew him—Banghart. Then, there is Casimir Wuldfache."

"Yes. This mysterious Casimir Wuldfache. Who is he?"

"He is a component of one of the strangest coincidences in human history. With trillions upon trillions of persons across the Gaean Reach, why should Casimir Wuldfache appear in two successive cases? I will enjoy talking to him. . . . Another matter occurs to me. If the Ubaikh destroy the Kzyk and their castle, then Istagam will also be destroyed—whereupon my responsibilities on Maz are dissolved."

"And then you'd be leaving? With poor Dirby in the Exhibitory?"

"Naturally, that matter would have to be clarified. . . . I can't understand the purpose of those wooden towers. They must be offensive machines of some sort."

The great gantries were brought forward and ranged in a half-circle fifty yards from the Kzyk castle, and it could now be seen that they stood as tall as or taller than the outer towers. The strutting bands of Ubaikh formed themselves into rigid formations. On the castle parapets, the Kzyk stood quiet.

Janika hunched her shoulders. "I don't think I'm tele-pathic . . . but something is happening that I can almost feel, or hear. . . . it's as if they're singing, or reciting some terrible ode."

"There go the Ubaikh up the towers."

"They're the flyers. On the top platform they'll strap on their wings. The Kzyk are waiting."

The Kzyk flew first. Over the parapets, launched by some invisible device, came a dark shape soaring on wings of black membrane. The flyer convulsed his legs, kicked; the wings twisted and flapped; the flyer swung in an arc, to gain altitude where the west wind was deflect-ed upward by the castle wall and a curving ramp below.

Another Kzyk flyer darted into the sky, and another and another; seven flyers soared in the air current hurled aloft by the ramp.

One of these now laid back his wings and darted down upon a Ubaikh captain. From the Ubaikh ranks came a rising scream. The captain swung around, apprised him-self of his peril. He seized a lance, butted it into the soil, and pointed it toward the Kzyk, who wheeled away and soared off into the upflow of air and presently regained his altitude.

The Ubaikh flyers launched themselves from their towers and entered the updraft; in the air over the par-apets occurred a dozen small battles, each flyer hacking at the body or the head of his adversary, but never at the vulnerable wings. Occasionally a pair grappled, tearing and stabbing at each other, to topple slowly head-over-heels toward the ground in a fluttering, flapping con-fusion of arms, legs and wings, disengaging at the last possible instant, and sometimes not at all.

Ubaikh flyers landed upon the parapets to do battle with the Kzyk defenders; others settled upon the but-tresses joining the outer towers to the keep, where the Kzyk struggled to thrust them off.

For an hour the air battle raged; the Kzyk defenders repelling the Ubaikh attackers, and the sward became littered with corpses. The wind was rising; the flyers soared and wheeled, rising to great heights, then lunging upon their opponents.

Tattered clouds began to fleet across the sky; in the west a bank of black clouds flared with lightning. The flyers were hurled downwind, toppling head-over-heels, and no more flyers were launched. The Ubaikh warriors clambered up, swarmed across the buttresses, leaped down upon the parapets. From the towers, the Kzyk counter-attacked, toppling the gantries to the ground. Battles raged along the parapets, then all the Ubaikh were torn apart, and their corpses thrown to the ground.

From a cloud overhead a spout of white light struck the Kzyk castle; another, then a third; three smoking holes gaped into the structure, and Kzyk came swarming forth like frantic insects.

Janika gasped. "What terrible lightning!"

Hetzel stared in wonder up at the cloud that had discharged such awesome bolts of energy. From the corner of his eye he glimpsed motion; he looked to where a black air car floated over the crest of the hill. It spat a projectile into the cloud, then darted aside and away.

The cloud flickered to a blast of internal orange fire; down like a dead bird dropped a black hull, twisted and burned. The design was strange to Hetzel. He looked at Janika.

"The Liss patrol boat."

Within the Liss craft, backup mechanisms took effect; the boat slid out of its fall and swerved off to the west. From its bow came another spout of white dazzle; the air car was outlined and coruscations fell behind the hill. The Liss ship limped off to the west. It jerked ahead, stopped short, then turned up its stern and jerked down at great speed, to bury itself into the hillside.

The Ubaikh and Kzyk were now fighting a desperate war, from which all gallantry and punctilio had disappeared. Out from the castle swarmed hundreds of Kzyk, outnumbering the Ubaikh by two to one; the Ubaikh fell back.

"Here comes the transport from Axistil," said Janika in a faint voice.

The carrier descended from the sky to the landing. A pair of Kzyk disembarked, to examine the combat and the ravaged castle with calm and critical gazes.

Hetzel, Janika, and the Ubaikh chieftain boarded the carrier. Hetzel went to speak to the pilot. The carrier rose from the depot, and at Hetzel's direction slid low over the hill. The air car lay smoldering on the turf. Hetzel and the pilot jumped to the ground and went to inspect the wreck. Inside the cage of twisted metal could be seen a body: contorted, burned, but still recognizable —a man Hetzel had never seen but knew very well. "So much for Casimir Wuldfache," said Hetzel. "He died for Istagam."

CHAPTER 12

The carrier flew north along the shore of the Frigid Ocean, then swung southwest, flying through the night, while Hetzel and Janika dozed and the Ubaikh chieftain sat sternly erect. At dawn the carrier arrived at the Axistil depot, at the far corner of the Plaza. Four Gomaz passengers alighted, then the Ubaikh, finally Hetzel and Janika, limping with fatigue. "Civilization," said Hetzel. "Axistil is the end of nowhere, but right now it looks like home. Are you coming to the Beyranion for breakfast? Your old friend Gidion Dirby will be on hand."

Janika made a wry grimace. "I don't want to see Gidion Dirby. Roseland Residential is just yonder. First I'm going to take a hot bath, then I'll resign from the tourist agency, and then I'm going to bed for the rest of the day. I hope Zaressa hasn't used all the hot water."

"Tonight, then, at the Beyranion."

"Thank you for the wonderful time. And I'll see you tonight."

Hetzel watched her until she turned down the Avenue of Lost Souls.

The Ubaikh stamped and hissed, a formidable spectacle in his five-pronged cast-iron helmet, black vest studded with iron bosses, and dangling black iron sword. Hetzel spoke into the translator. "Today should

125

see the finish of this unpleasant affair, which will gratify all of us except the assassins."

The Ubaikh replied; the printout read: "Aliens are overtimorous. They fear death. They lack patriotism." The word "patriotism" was printed in red and underlined, to indicate approximation. "Why waste so much anguish over a few killings, especially since those expunged were not your own kind?"

"The situation is more complex than you imagine," said Hetzel. "In any event, your part in this matter will soon be accomplished, and you will be at liberty to return to your castle."

"The sooner the better. Let us proceed."

"We must wait an hour or two."

"Another example of Gaean frivolity. All night we hurtle through the air at great speed in order to arrive at Axistil; now you delay. The Gomaz are direct and precise."

"Delay is sometimes unavoidable. I will take you to the famous Beyranion Hotel, a lavish castle of the Gaeans, where I intend to honor you with a gift or two." He set off across the Plaza. The Ubaikh uttered a peevish hiss and strode after him, irons clanking, and so purposefully that Hetzel cringed back in alarm; then, recovering his poise, he turned and led the way to the Beyranion, where, to his relief, no one was yet astir.

Making sounds of reluctance and distaste, the Ubaikh entered Hetzel's rooms. Gidion Dirby was nowhere to be seen; Hetzel was hardly surprised. Dirby, in his present frame of mind, must be considered unpredictable.

Hetzel motioned to the couch. "Rest upon this piece of furniture. I have decided to offer you several gifts, to compensate for your inconvenience." He went to his luggage and brought forth a hand lamp and an assault knife with a proteum edge. Hetzel explained the operation of the lamp and gave a warning in regard to the knife. "Take great care. The edge is invisible; it will cut anything it touches. You can slice your iron sword as if it were a withe."

The Ubaikh uttered sibilant sounds. The printout read: "This is an act of appeasement, which has been noted with approval."

Gomaz for "thanks," thought Hetzel. He said, "I now plan to bathe and change my garments. As soon as possible thereafter, we will transact our business."

"I am impatient to depart without delay."

"There will be as little delay as possible. Rest yourself. Please do not test the knife upon the furnishings of this room. Do you want to look at a picture book?"

"Negative."

Hetzel, clean and in fresh garments, returned to the sitting room. The Ubaikh apparently had not shifted position. Hetzel asked, "Do you require food or refreshment?"

"Negative."

Hetzel dropped into a chair. The hot water had worked to soporific effect; his eyelids drooped. He looked at his watch: At least an hour until he could expect to find Sir Estevan at the Triskelion. He spoke into the translator. "Why did the Ubaikh attack the Kzyk in a 'war of hate'?"

"The Kzyk have allied themselves with the Gaeans. They have agreed to an ignoble collaboration, in return for supplies of 'manstuff'—printed in red, to indicate paraphrase of an untranslatable word—"and the Gaeans teach them to construct energy weapons. In five years the Kzyk will roam Maz in overpowering hordes; their bantlings will carry guns and fly like gargoyles and destroy our bantlings; the Kzyk will dominate the world, unless the Ubaikh destroy them now, alone, or in coalition with other loyal septs."

"And what is 'man-stuff'?"

"I have spoken enough to the Gaean enemy. I will say no more."

Hetzel sat back in the chair. Where was Gidion Dirby? If the Liss or the Olefract were aware of his identity—and according to Sir Estevan, they knew everything that transpired both at the Triskelion and at the Beyranion Hotel—then Gidion Dirby might well encounter unpleasantness in Dogtown. Or even at the Beyranion itself, which was by no means invulnerable to intrusion, as Hetzel himself could testify. Dirby might have been sleep-gassed and taken away, never to be seen again.

The telephone chimed. Hetzel jerked up from the chair. He touched buttons; Janika looked forth from the screen. Her face was haggard with fatgue and horror. She spoke in a husky voice. "Vv. Byrrhis is dead! There have been thieves!"

"Where are you calling from?"

"I'm at the agency."

"What are you doing there?"

"I came down to quit my job; I want to leave Axistil. I don't care about the money, and Vv. Byrrhis is lying dead on the floor." Her voice rose a quavering octave.

Hetzel thought a moment. "How was he killed?"

"I don't know."

"How do you know thieves were responsible?"

"The safe is open; his wallet is on the floor."

"And there's no money left?"

"Nothing, so far as I can see. What should I do?"

"I suppose you'd better call the Dogtown marshall. There's not much else you can do."

"I don't want to be involved; I don't want to answer questions; I just want to run away and leave."

"The old man in the curio shop undoubtedly saw you

arrive, and if you don't make a report, they'll think you're involved. Call the marshal and tell the truth. You have nothing to hide."

"That's true. Very well. I wish you were here representing me instead of Gidion Dirby."

"I'll finish with Dirby today, and Istagam as well, or so I hope. Then I can devote my full attention to you."

"Unless I'm in the Dogtown jail."

"I'll telephone you as soon as I finish at the Triskelion. If I can't get you at home or the agency, I'll try the jail. You'd better call the marshal right now."

Janika gave a wan assent, and the screen went blank. Hetzel turned around, to see Gidion Dirby coming in through the door. He stopped short, looking in bemusement from Hetzel to the Ubaikh.

"Who's this?" asked Dirby. "A new client?"

Hetzel made no reply. Dirby came further into the room. Hetzel thought that he seemed flushed and excited, tumescent with some unidentifiable emotion. Pride? Triumph? Hetzel asked sourly, "How much did you take from him?"

Dirby jerked back a bit, as if he had encountered an invisible wall. He attempted carelessness. "From whom?"

"Byrrhis."

Dirby's mouth sagged a trifle, then curved into a tight smile. "You mean Banghart."

"Whatever his name is."

"Worried about your fee?"

"Not at all."

"Perhaps you should be worried. You haven't done much."

"First of all," said Hetzel, "I listened to you. Second, I prevented Aeolus Shult from turnng you over to Captain Baw. Third, I've found a witness to the assassinations." He nodded toward the Ubaikh. "If you're innocent, he'll testify as much. So, once again: how much did you take from Byrrhis, or Banghart?"

"It's not really your affair," said Dirby. "Whatever I took, he owes me."

"Two thousand SLU is the receptionist's salary. A thousand is my fee. The rest of the money, I'm not concerned about."

"Dirby's face became sullen. "The rest doesn't amount to very much. What do I get out of all this? Don't forget, I have a claim too!"

"Need I remind you," said Hetzel, "that this 'claim' is what you hoped to earn from your smuggling activities? And that you've just murdered a man to gain control of the money?"

"I murdered no one," snapped Dirby. "I was walking down the street; I looked into the tourist agency, and there was Banghart, big as life. I went in, and one word led to another. He went for his gun and I twisted his neck. I won and took the money he was carrying."

Hetzel waited.

Reluctantly Dirby said, "It was a bit more than five thousand."

Hetzel waited.

Dirby growled under his breath and brought forth his wallet. He counted out notes, tossed them on the table. "There's three thousand. Pay off the receptionist; the rest is your fee."

"Thank you," said Hetzel. "By now Sir Estevan will be at the Triskelion, and we will undertake to clarify the circumstances of the assassinations."

Hetzel went to the telephone, punched buttons. The screen became decorated with the flower-petal face of Zaressa Lurling. Hetzel heard Gidion Dirby mutter in amazement.

"Connect me, please, with Sir Estevan."

Zaressa's face became professionally blank. "Sir

Estevan is occupied; he won't be able to see you today."

"Tell him Vv. Hetzel wants to speak to him; tell him that the Ubaikh who witnessed the assassinations is on hand and has agreed to provide information."

Zaressa's mouth quavered in uncertainty. "I'm not supposed to bother Sir Estevan; why not discuss the matter later in the day with Captain Baw?"

"Young woman," said Hetzel, "I am calling at Sir Estevan's own express request! Connect me at once!"

"I can't interrupt him now. He's busy with Captain Baw."

"You must interrupt him because I'm now on my way to the Triskelion, with Gidion Dirby and the Ubaikh. We will arrive in five minutes, and Sir Estevan is anxious to see us." Hetzel flicked off the screen and blew out his breath. "I've never seen such obduracy! Is she a machine? Does Sir Estevan beat her when she makes a mistake? Is she determined to insulate Sir Estevan from the realities of life? Is she simply stupid?"

"I've seen that girl before," said Gidion Dirby in a thick voice. "Sometimes, when I was a captive, I'd wake up to find a girl crawling around the room on her hands and knees. This was the girl."

"Really!" said Hetzel. "How can you be sure? The girl wore a domino, I thought you said."

"I still recognize her."

Hetzel made a sound of annoyance. "We want fewer complications, not more."

"It's not necessarily a complication."

"Perhaps not. After all, Sir Estevan was filmed in the corridor of his private villa, no doubt by Byrrhis. . . . Well, let's get on with our principal business."

Dirby rubbed his chin thoughtfully. "Perhaps I'd better wait here until matters are settled. I don't care to risk Captain Baw."

"If you're innocent, you don't need to worry."

"Oh, I'm innocent, no fear of that."

"Then you must come. I want to set up conditions exactly as they were—"

"A reenactment."

"A reenactment, precisely."

Dirby shrugged. "Just as you say. If Captain Baw claps me into the Exhibitory, you've got to get me out." He walked toward the door. Hetzel stepped forward, grappled Dirby with one arm, felt in Dirby's pouch with the other, and withdrew a gun. Dirby wrenched himself free, face contorted. He started to fling himself upon Hetzel; then, seeing Hetzel's face—the arrogant, down-drooping mouth, the cold gray gaze—and noting the gun held negligently ready, he backed away.

Hetzel said politely, "I merely want to make sure that I, not you, control the situation. Come along, then."

CHAPTER 13

The three walked across the vast gray-silver Plaza.
The sun hung halfway up the green sky; the day seemed
clearer than usual, and the eccentric architecture of the
Triskelion was manifest.

Vvs. Felius and Vv. Kylo stood on duty behind the
Gaean desk. Vvs. Felius, observing Gidion Dirby and
the Ubaikh, leaned back with bulging eyes and a trembling jaw. Hetzel went directly to Sir Estevan's office.
Vvs. Felius called out indignantly, but Hetzel paid no
attention.

Sir Estevan himself stood in the outer office, standing
by Zaressa's desk with his hand on her shoulder.
Zaressa's face was pink and her eyes were wet. Sir
Estevan appeared to be consoling her. He looked at
Hetzel with unsympathetic eyes. "I can't quite condone
your hectoring of my secretary."

"She has exaggerated my offense," said Hetzel. "I did
no more than insist upon seeing you. I have here the
Ubaikh who witnessed the assassinations, and here is
Gidion Dirby, who was also present. Hopefully, we will
be able to discover the truth of the situation."

Sir Estevan seemed uninterested in Hetzel's remarks.
"Quite frankly, I'm bored with the whole matter. So far
as I'm concerned, the matter can rest in abeyance."

Gidion Dirby uttered a caw of savage laughter. "I
don't want to let the matter rest! You accused me and

133

sent your pet porpoise out to arrest me; let's hear what
the witness has to say."

Sir Estevan gazed at Dirby without expression, then
turned to Hetzel. "I have just received news that Vv.
Byrrhis has been murdered. What do you know of this?"

"I am an effectuator," said Hetzel. "If you want me to
perform an investigation, I may or may not be able to
help you, depending upon the fee. Vv. Dirby hired me to
bring the facts of the Triskelion assassinations to light,
and this is my single concern. I suggest that you summon Captain Baw. We can then step into the chamber
and allow the Ubaikh to indicate the source of the
shots."

Sir Estevan gave a stony shurg. "I don't care to partic-
ipate in any such demonstration. The Liss and the
Olefract are the aggrieved parties. Perform your demonstrations before them."

"In that case," cried Dirby, "why did you send Baw
to arrest me?"

"Captain Baw undertook the arrest on his own in-
itiative."

"As I see the situation," said Hetzel, "the Liss and the
Olefract Triarchs were killed because they were about to
hear a complaint against Istagam, which they would
have been only too glad to act upon. Given the circumstances of Gidion Dirby's detention and your unwilling-
ness to investigate the matter, I believe that Gidion
Dirby has grounds for legal action. Unless you cooper-
ate now, it will appear that you are attempting to cover
up for Istagam, presumably because you are profiting
from the operation."

"Totally false," said Sir Estevan. "As I may have remarked to you, Istagam is an altruistic enterprise organized by Vv. Byrrhis. The Gomaz work productively
instead of killing each other; they learn the rudiments of
civilized knowledge in return. Istagam profits have built
the magnificent tourist-agency inns. Neither I nor Vv.

Byrrhis have cause for shame."

Dirby said brassily, "Don't be too sure of that. Who turned the chamber pot over my head? Do you think I've forgotten? Not much! Give me the opportunity, and I'll do the same for you."

Sir Estevan gave a snort of chilly humor. "I suggest that you keep a civil tongue in your head. You're now in the jurisdiction of the Triarchy; I can easily turn you over to the Liss and the Olefract, and you can vent your impudence upon them."

"You would certainly be exceeding your authority," said Hetzel. "Either you, as the Gaean Triarch, are aggrieved, or you are not aggrieved. You can't have it both ways. If you are not aggrieved, you have no right to inconvenience Vv. Dirby."

"If nothing else," said Sir Estevan, "the Gaeans have suffered embarrassment and ruinous loss of face. At the minimum, I am justified in believing that Dirby attempted murder upon me."

"This is sheer speculation."

"Captain Baw was witness to the circumstance."

"Suppose, for the sake of argument, that Captain Baw shot the Triarchs himself. He would then be certain to blame the crime upon Gidion Dirby; do you agree?"

"Ridiculous," said Sir Estevan. "Why should Baw kill the Triarchs?"

"The same question applies to Dirby. Why should he kill the Triarchs?"

"I couldn't say. Perhaps he is deranged."

"So you want to arrest a crazy man and turn him over to the Liss and the Olefract?"

Sir Estevan showed signs of boredom. "Criminality is a kind of insanity; criminals are punished under Gaean law; hence, under Gaean law, insane persons suffer punishment. How crazy is Dirby? I have no idea. He looks sane enough now."

"So does Captain Baw. So do you. No doubt the Ubaikh appears sane."

"Exactly what are you suggesting?" demanded Sir Estevan.

"I suggest that you look before you leap. Have you spoken to Vv. Dirby; have you heard his account?"

"No; it is really irrelevant. The facts are as they are."

"Vv. Dirby," said Hetzel, "be good enough to repeat to Sir Estevan what you told me."

Dirby gave his head a mulish shake. "Let him put me under arrest, I'll tell my tale in court, and let him squirm."

"If you don't tell him," said Hetzel, "I will."

"Do as you like; it's the same to me."

Hetzel said, "As accurately as I can recall, these are the circumstances." He presented a brief outline of Dirby's experiences. "It is clear that Vv. Dirby is a victim rather than a criminal. The question becomes: who in actual fact is the assassin? We can resolve the mystery in ten minutes, and it seems important to do so."

"Important to whom?" inquired Sir Estevan in a cool voice. "As I say, the grievance is not mine."

"The grievance is mine!" snarled Dirby. "For all I know, you're the murderer yourself. I'll get the Gaean marshal in and turn all the facts over to him!"

Sir Estevan threw up his arms in a fatalistic gesture. "Very well, let's make an end to it." He stepped into the lobby and signaled Captain Baw, who stood in glowering colloquy with Vvs. Felius. All marched into the Chamber of Triarchs. Sir Estevan went to the chair of the Gaean Triarch. "Captain Baw, please dispose these people as before."

"Very well. The Ubaikh stood here. Over here . . . come stand here, there's a good lad! I'd just come in through the side door with Dirby. He was about here, and I'd started across the room. I was about here when I heard the sound of shots." He addressed Sir Estevan. "Would this accord with your recollection, sir?"

"Yes." Sir Estevan seemed limp and dispirited. "Close enough."

"Close enough," said Dirby.

Hetzel spoke to the Ubaikh through the translator. "This is approximately the state of affairs when the shots were fired. Do you agree?"

The printout read: "I agree."

"Very well, then—who fired the shots?"

Hetzel read the printout. "He says he doesn't know."

" 'He doesn't know'! I thought you said he would testify!"

Hetzel spoke to the Ubaikh. "Explain your remark, if you will. You heard the shots; you saw where they came from—but you can't specify the individual who fired them?"

"The shots came from here." The Ubaikh indicated the door leading into Sir Estevan's private office. "The door opened; the shots were fired; the door was shut. I have told you what I know, and I will now return to the Ubaikh domain." He stalked from the chamber.

Dirby uttered a shout of vindictive glee. He took a step toward Captain Baw, but Hetzel interposed himself. "You are now exculpated," said Hetzel. "You are free to come and go. Why not return to Thrope and rest for a period? You have had a harrowing experience."

Dirby grinned. "Quite correct, and no doubt I'll do just that." He darted a final glance toward Sir Estevan, then turned on his heel and left the chamber.

"And now—from sheer curiosity—who was in your office?"

"When I left, the office was empty."

"In that case, Zaressa Lurling would seem to be the guilty individual."

"Impossible! Can you imagine her aiming and firing a gun?"

Hetzel shrugged. "Stranger things have happened. You had no inkling of this?"

Sir Estevan made no response. He looked toward his

office. "I suppose now we must pursue the matter to its bitter limit." He went to the door, thrust it aside. Zaressa Lurling was nowhere to be seen. Vvs. Felius sat at the reception desk. "Zaressa became ill," said Vvs. Felius. "She asked me to take her place and went home."

Sir Estevan stood stiff and rigid. Hetzel asked, "Vvs. Felius, do you recall the events just prior to the assassination?"

"I certainly do."

"Did Vv. Byrrhis, or anyone else, go into Sir Estevan's office?"

"Absolutely not. No one came but yourself and that Dirby fellow."

"Thank you. I don't think you need remain any longer."

Vvs. Felius gave Hetzel a glare and looked at Sir Estevan. "Do you need me, Sir Estevan?"

"No, thank you, Vvs. Felius. You may go."

Vvs. Felius haughtily left the room. Sir Estevan sat heavily down in a chair.

"So, then . . . Zaressa either fired the shots, or else she admitted the assassin through your private entrance. As to her motives we can only speculate. In any event, she shares the guilt of the murderer, either Wuldfache or Byrrhis. His identity is irrelevant; both are dead. I suspect Wuldfache, and I assume that Zaressa was enamored of him."

"Yes," groaned Sir Estevan. "No doubt. . . . I admit that I suspected her guilt . . . and I did not care to learn the truth."

"You apparently take a more than casual interest in Zaressa Lurling."

"This is nothing that concerns you."

"As you say, the matter is irrelevant. Byrrhis was the architect of the affair. He understood the enormous profits latent in Istagam, even over a relevantly short period. He also knew that opposition was sure to materialize from you, from the Liss and Olefract Triarchs, or from all three. He prepared to neutralize the opposition, and brought Dirby to Maz. In order for Dirby to appear a convincing assassin, he must be supplied with motivation, hence his processing, which Byrrhis no doubt found amusing. He was aided by Casimir Wuldfache, whose adventures are a saga in themselves.

"At the old Kanitze castle, Dirby was conditioned, and his mind loaded with a whole catalog of insane events. But Dirby himself was *not* insane and could emphatically affirm the reality of these events. The more he asserted, the more insane he would seem; any alienist would declare him hyperparanoid. Even better, his ravings would be corroborated by mind search, which, after all, gauges only subjective authenticity.

"So, then: Byrrhis has contrived a subtle, complex but flexible plan. If and when complaints are made in regard to Istagam, the Liss and Olefract Triarchs will be killed, and Istagam is given another year, perhaps longer; and Sir Estevan becomes a person who by a hair's breadth has escaped assassination at the hands of a paranoid wanderer.

"But what of Sir Estevan? He must also be induced to ignore the activities of Istagam. Sir Estevan is a proud and obstinate man. How can he be so persuaded? He must be subjected to blackmail. Conditions have now been created whereby Sir Estevan can convincingly appear to be nefarious, base, and foolish. If he jibs or balks, Byrrhis, safely in Dogtown or off-planet, makes public the circumstances surrounding the assassinations and claims Sir Estevan to be his collaborator. Dirby's hallucinations are certified as reality. *You*, Sir Estevan, have performed these absurd tricks, *you* have turned the chamber pot over Dirby's head, and *you* become a figure of contempt and ridicule across the Gaean Reach; your dignity and reputation are lost forever. Hence, you are in no position to thwart Vv. Byrrhis' schemes."

For a moment Sir Estevan's face remained still—a

mask, classically handsome, the golden hair curling down upon his ears, the chin strong and set. What transpired behind the mask, Hetzel could only guess. Sir Estevan might be possessed of a honed and intricate intelligence, or he might be blank and dull.

"Remarkable," said Sir Estevan coldly. "But I am not so concerned with public 'contempt and ridicule' as you suppose. Secondly, the Kzyk have lost their zest for knowledge. They are not interested in orthography and double-entry bookkeeping; they want guns and pulsors and machinery to level their enemies' castles, which Byrrhis, for all his cleverness, dared not supply."

"Byrrhis was ready to supply a commodity equally valuable," said Hetzel. "Virility hormone—*chir*. He brought down a cargo of chemical, which now is stored in Kanitze castle, unless I am much mistaken. The Kzyk would work without cessation for this material; *chir* is the stuff they value most. Indeed, Byrrhis imported such a remarkable quantity of the material, I suspect that he planned to establish a whole chain of Istagams across the various continents. A year or two of such enterprise, and Vv. Byrrhis could retire a very wealthy man indeed."

Sir Estevan turned away. "I don't care to hear any more."

"From sheer curiosity—what will you do with Zaressa Lurling?"

"I will ask her to leave Maz on the next ship and never return. The crime was not committed against a Gaean, and I can do no more, even if I wanted to do so."

CHAPTER 14

Hetzel returned across the glimmering gray Plaza to the Beyranion Hotel. He had achieved his goals; he had earned an adequate fee, but the circumstances provided him no great satisfaction. For the hundredth time he wondered about the quality of his profession. Were greed, hate, lust, and cruelty to disappear, there would be little work for effectuators. . . . Maz was by no means a cheerful world. He would be relieved to see it dwindle astern.

In the Beyranion dining room he took an early lunch, then went to his rooms and telephoned the spaceport. The *Zanthine*, a packet of the Argo Navis Line, departed Axistil on the morrow; Hetzel made reservations for passage.

He poured himself a goblet of Baltranck cordial, added a splash of soda. Dirby, so he noted, had made valiant inroads upon the flask during his sojourn. Well, why not? A surly fellow, Gidion Dirby, who had learned neither wisdom nor tolerance nor generosity from his vicissitudes: the usual order of things. Tragedy was not necessarily ennobling; travail weakened the soul more often than it gave strength. On the whole, Dirby might be considered an average human being. Hetzel decided that he bore Dirby no ill will. Casimir

Wuldfache/Byrrhis? Hetzel felt emotion neither one way nor the other. His mood, he thought, was extraordinarily flat. Since the confrontation at the Triskelion he had done nothing but brood. The explanation, of course, was obvious: fatigue and numbness after the events at Black Cliff Inn, in the Shimkish Mountains, on the Steppe of Long Bones. As he sat sipping the cordial, the circumstances seemed fragile and unreal, dreams.

A chime at the door announced a visitor. Hetzel slid to the sideboard, took up his weapon, and looked around at the windows. Visits in the aftermath of cases often presaged dire happenings. He went sidling and wary to the door, touched the viewplate, to reveal the face of Sir Estevan Tristo.

Hetzel slid the door aside. Sir Estevan came slowly into the room. He presented, thought Hetzel, a most untypical and dispirited appearance. His skin showed the color of putty; his yellow hair seemed wilted. Without waiting for an invitation, Sir Estevan lowered himself into a chair. Hetzel poured a second goblet of Baltranck and soda and handed it to Sir Estevan.

"Thank you." Sir Estevan swirled the liquid around the glass and stared down into the cusps of reflected light. He looked up at Hetzel. "You wonder why I am here."

"Not at all. You want to talk to me."

Sir Estevan showed a wan smile and tasted the cordial. "Quite true. As you divined, I took an extraordinary interest in Zaressa, and now I find myself in a rather maudlin state. Life now seems very grim, very grim indeed."

"I can appreciate this," said Hetzel. "Zaressa was a most charming creature."

Sir Estevan set the goblet upon the table. "Byrrhis encountered her at Twisselbane on Tamar, apparently under rather sordid circumstances. He sent her out here and recommended that I give her a job. I became enamored; I transferred Vvs. Felius to the reception desk and installed Zaressa as my secretary, and she quickly made herself indispensable. Meanwhile, of course, she was plotting with the unspeakable Byrrhis." Sir Estevan picked up the goblet and drank. "But now, poor thing, I forgive her everything; she is paying very dearly for her offense."

"Indeed? I thought you had merely instructed her to leave Maz."

"So I did; this was her intention. I should have mentioned to you that Liss and Olefract both are able to eavesdrop on my offices. They knew as soon as we that Zaressa was involved in the assassinations. Zaressa went to her rooms to pack. She was accosted by two men, taken to a vehicle, and delivered to the Liss. Her roommate communicated with me; I made an urgent protest, but to no avail. They sent her away in a Liss ship. She'll never see another human being in whatever span of life remains to her."

Hetzel made a small grimace. Both men sat quiet, watching colors shift and change in their goblets.

Sir Estevan had departed. Hetzel sat for a period in silent reflection. Then he telephoned the Roseland Residence. Janika was not in her rooms. Hetzel wondered as to where she might be.

Five minutes later she rang the chime at his door. Hetzel let her in. Her eyes were red, her face was swollen with tears. "Have you heard what happened to Zaressa?"

Hetzel put his arm around her shoulder and stroked her hair. "Sir Estevan told me."

"I want to leave Maz; I never want to come back."

"There's a packet leaving tomorrow. I reserved passage for you."

"Thank you. Where does it take us?"

"Where do you want to go?"

"I don't know. Anywhere."

"That can easily be arranged." Hetzel lifted the flask that once had contained Baltranck and that now was dry. "Do you care for an aperitif? We can sit out in the garden and have the waiter bring us something refreshing."

"That sounds pleasant. Let me go wash my face. I'm sure I look ridiculous. But when I think of Zaressa, I go to pieces."

They sat at a table where they could watch the glittering flakelet of a sun drift down the sky. Across the Plaza the Triskelion loomed through the murk. "This is a terrible world," said Janika. "I'll never forget it; I'll never be gay and careless again. Do you know, it might as easily have been me as Zaressa; I might easily have done just what she did. How would she know that Casimir Wuldfache planned to shoot the Triarchs?"

"So . . . Vv. Byrrhis wasn't guilty after all."

Janika gave a scornful laugh. "He'd never have taken the risk. And Zaressa would never have opened the door for him. For Casimir Wuldfache she'd do anything. Even in Twisselbane she yearned for him. He preferred me; I couldn't tolerate him, and so both Casimir and Zaressa hated me."

"Cassimir Wuldfache, oddly enough, is responsible for my being here now."

"Oh? How so?"

"At first I thought it a coincidence, but now—"

Footsteps sounded; Gidion Dirby sauntered up the path. He gave an astounded gasp and stopped short, staring at Janika with eyes bulging from his face. "What are you doing here?"

CHAPTER 15

As before, Sir Ivon Hacaway received Hetzel on the terrace of Harth Manor. Hetzel had already presented a brief report by telephone, and Sir Ivon's manner was far more affable than on the previous occasion.

Hetzel described his activities in detail and rendered his expense account, in regard to which Sir Ivon gave a rueful smile. "My honor, but you do yourself well!"

"I saw no need to stint," said Hetzel. "I do high-quality work under high-quality conditions. There remains a single matter to discuss—the bonus that you offered for decisive effectuation. Istagam is no longer in existence, and nothing could be more definite than this."

Sir Ivon's face clouded. "I hardly see the need for any larger outlay."

"As you wish. I can earn a rather smaller sum by writing an article for the micronics trade journal, describing the possibilities for a new, better-organized Istagam. After all, it never was and is not now illegal to employ Gomaz labor, and *chir* is cheap."

Sir Ivon gave a weary sigh and brought out his checkbook. "A thousand SLU will be sufficient, and I will make it my business to see that *chir* is declared contraband."

"Two thousand would better convey your appreciation. However, I'll settle for fifteen hundred, and I believe that Sir Estevan Tristo has already placed an embargo on *chir*. Still . . ."

Sir Ivon glumly wrote the check. Hetzel expressed gratitude, wished Sir Ivon good health, and took his leave. He went to the front of the manor, rang the chime, and when the footman opened the door, requested a word with Lady Bonvenuta. He was conducted into the library, where Lady Bonvenuta shortly appeared. At the sight of Hetzel she halted, raised her eyebrows. "Yes?"

"I am Miro Hetzel, to whom a friend of yours, a certain Madame X, entrusted a trifle of confidential business."

Lady Bonventura touched her lips with the tip of her tongue. "I'm afraid I know of no such Madame X."

"She was anxious to locate a gentleman by the name of Casimir Wuldfache, and I am pleased to report that I have details on his personal whereabouts."

"Indeed?" Her voice was more frosty than ever.

"First, I must inform you that Casimir Wuldfache took advantage of Madame X and her friendship with you and rifled Sir Ivon's file of private papers. This will come as a great shock to you."

"Why, yes. Of course. But, then . . . well, I think I know the Madame X to whom you refer. She will want to learn where this Casimir Wuldfache can be found."

"The information reached me as an incidental to another effectuation, and I will not require payment, especially as Casimir Wuldfache is dead."

"Dead!" Lady Bonvenuta blinked and clutched at a chair with bejeweled fingers.

"Dead as a doornail. I myself saw his corpse on the Steppe of Long Bones, north of Axistil, on the planet Maz, where he had been engaged in business. May I ask you a question?"

"This is shocking news! What is your question?"

"A rather trivial matter. Did you recommend me to Sir Ivon, or did he remark to you that I was an efficient and dependable effectuator?"

"I heard him discuss you with one of his friends, and I passed the recommendation on to Madame X."

"Thank you," said Hetzel. "The chain of circumstances is now complete. My best regards to Madame X, and I hope that the news regarding Vv. Wuldfache will not distress her."

"I hardly think so. It was a matter of business. I will telephone her at this minute. Good day, Vv. Hetzel."

"Good day, Lady Bonvenuta. It has been a pleasure to meet you."

Part Two:
Freitzke's Turn

CHAPTER 1

Arriving at Cassander on the world Thesse, Hetzel lodged himself at the Hotel of the Worlds, using a fictitious name. After a bath and a meal he seated himself at the communicator, called for and secured a certified channel, guaranteed safe from interference. He touched buttons, spoke a code word, and the screen displayed his personal emblem: a skull with the Tree of Life growing up from one of the eye sockets. His own voice spoke: "Office of Miro Hetzel, Effectuator."

"I will consult anyone on the premises," Hetzel replied, though the premises, as he well knew, included no more than a few circuits at Cassander Communications Center.

"The premises are vacant," stated the familiar voice. "Miro Hetzel is not immediately available. Please leave a message."

"Two six two six. Miro Hetzel here. Transmit messages."

Assured by code and voice analysis that Hetzel himself had issued the demand, the reception system yielded its file of messages, dating from Hetzel's previous departure from Cassander. Much of the matter was trivial. There were two threats, three warnings, four demands for money. A few, spoken in guarded or disguised voices, or in rambling, only half-coherent sentences, fit no pattern, but to these Hetzel listened with careful attention: they contained intimations too troubling to be articulated clearly. Hetzel heard nothing which he considered of urgent importance.

The remainder of the messages, seven in all, solicited Hetzel's services. None supplied informative detail. Three made use of the phrase: "Money is of no object," or "Expense is secondary to results." Hetzel suspected that several applicants wished to be delivered from blackmail, an operation at which he had been notably successful in the past. Other offers could not so readily be classified. To all the reception system, after extracting all possible information, delivered the message: "Miro Hetzel is presently off-world. If you fail to receive a response within three days, we recommend the Extran Effectuation Service, whose integrity and skill are of a high order."

The last message in the system's memory had been received three days previously almost to the minute; and this message also was that which aroused in Hetzel the keenest interest. He listened to it a second time: "You do not know me; my name is Clent—Conwit Clent. My address is Dandyl Villa, Tangent Road, Junis. I am faced with a most troublesome problem—at least it seems troublesome to me. You may find it ludicrous. I might not have called you except that the affair concerns a certain Faurence Dacre, and your name happens to enter the case. Only at the periphery, I hasten to say. I repeat that the matter is most important and expense, within reason, is no object. I know your reputation and I hope you will be able to consult with me as soon as possible."

Hetzel immediately put through a call to Conwit Clent, at Dandyl Villa in the pleasant hillside suburb of Junis.

The face of Conwit Clent almost instantly appeared on the screen: a face which ordinarily must have seemed easy and generous, with curly blond hair, a well-shaped, if heavy nose, and a square block of a chin. The features now were drawn and pinched; the ruddy skin showed an unhealthy gray undertone.

Hetzel introduced himself. "Sorry for the delay. I arrived in town only an hour ago."

Clent's face sagged in relief. "Excellent! Can you come out to my home? Or would you prefer that I meet you in town?"

"Just a moment," said Hetzel. "Can you tell me something about your case?"

Clent cleared his throat and glanced over his shoulder. He muttered uncomfortably: "It's something difficult to discuss under any circumstances. You remember Faurence Dacre?"

"Certainly."

"Did you know that he became a surgeon?"

"I haven't seen or heard of him since he left school."

"Then you wouldn't know his present whereabouts?"

"No."

Clent sighed unhappily, not so much in response to Hetzel's remark, but as if certain dreary suppositions of his own had been fully confirmed. "If you'll come out to Dandyl Villa I'll explain everything in detail, and you'll appreciate my reasons for calling on you."

"Very well," said Hetzel. "I'll come at once. I must point out that my fees are calculated subjectively, and that I require prepayment sufficient to cover reasonable expenses."

Clent showed small interest in the subject. "We shall have no disputes in this regard."

As soon as the screen cleared, Hetzel called Extran Effectuations, with whom he maintained a friendly relationship, and was provided information from the Extran files. Conwit Clent was described as an unremarkable young man of wealth and good character, enthusiastic in regard to yachting, a dilettante at the collection of star stones*, and lately an aficionado of the complex Twair cuisine which currently enjoyed something of a mode among the young cognoscenti of Cassander. He had very recently married the beautiful Perdhra Olruff, from a family as wealthy as his own. His life had been void of scandal, hushed-up wrongdoing, or even irresponsiblity; Clent, so it seemed, had lived a blameless, secure, and unthreatened life. The photographs showed a man obviously healthy, with a head of blond curls and a mouth twisted into a curve of chronic good nature: a Conwit Clent similar to, yet indefinably different from, the Clent to whom Hetzel had so recently spoken. Perdhra Olruff was beyond a doubt a person of heartbreaking beauty: slender, dark-haired, with an innocent inquiring gaze, as if everywhere she sought to learn the elusive natural secrets. Her outlook upon life was perhaps more serious than that of Conwit Clent.

Hetzel next inquired for information in regard to Faurence Dacre, but discovered little. Dr. Dacre had arrived in Cassander only two years previously, but had immediately made a reputation as a brilliant and imaginative surgeon. Hetzel smiled grimly. Precisely the image which Faurence Dacre would have wished to make his own. And, taking all with all, why not? Faurence Dacre's skill, assurance, and intellectual powers fitted him well for such a career.

The file on Faurence Dacre contained nothing dark or sinister. In his brief two years at Cassander he had become something of a society darling, and his services were much in demand. He would have moved in approximately the same circles as Clent; inevitable that they should have become acquainted.

---

*Crystals occasionally discovered in the slag of dead stars.

Hetzel arose from the communicator, changed to a casual dark blue and gray lounge suit. He went out into the foyer, touched a button at the "Depart" chute. The gate slid ajar, Hetzel entered the capsule; the gates sealed themselves. Hetzel spoke into the mesh: "Dandyl Villa, Tangent Road, Junis." The capsule dropped, sought a route, and accelerated. Across the wall screens flashed a more or less accurate picture of the passing landscape: the black iron and glass of central Cassander, then the Park Belt, then the isolated little suburbs among the smokewoods, then the wide dense argents, flowering quains, cyan mimosas, and cardamoms which cloaked the Magnetic Hills, then up Junis Valley to the grand villas of Junis Town.

During the trip Hetzel thought back across his lifetime: an exercise provoked by the name "Faurence Dacre." There were more years than he cared to reckon. From Earth he had traveled with his family first to Alpheratz VI, where his father, a civil engineer, worked on the Great Tri-Ocean Canal, then to Neroli, where his mother had died in a Barking Desert windstorm, then a sorrowful rush through half a dozen places he barely remembered. On Thesse his father became supervisor of the Trembling Mountain Maintenance System, and there, at the Trembling Waters Academy, young Miro Hetzel had secured his formal education.

Miro Hetzel had been an unusual boy: strong, quick, and intelligent. While neither surly nor shy he was not naturally gregarious and slow to make friends. From his father he had learned self-reliance and practicality (or so he liked to think); his mother, a Gael from the Isle of Skye, had worked into young Miro's being a penchant for the subtle and mysterious. The two influences, rather than striving at discord, ran parallel to and reinforced each other (such was Miro's belief).

Without difficulty Miro encompassed the difficult curriculum at Trembling Waters Academy, and the years passed pleasantly. During his last term a new boy entered the school: Faurence Dacre, only recently arrived from the world Cambiasq, where, so he told, his father, Lord Icelyn Dacre, owned a large island and controlled the lives of a thousand people. Faurence Dacre was clearly a remarkable youth, as handsome as the Prince of Darkness, with hair like shining black silk, eyes like topazes illuminated from the side. He was tall, strong, agile, and intensely concentrated; he automatically excelled at sports. At Trembling Waters Academy, where almost all of the students excelled in one way or another, such capabilities aroused no particular comment, and Faurence Dacre strove more intensely than ever: more intensely and relentlessly, so it seemed to many, than circumstances might justify.

Academically, Faurence Dacre performed with contemptuous ease, as if the material were child's play, and again his abilities aroused no admiration; his single friend, indeed, was Miro Hetzel, who was tolerant enough to be amused by Faurence Dacre's antics. Miro occasionally counseled Faurence to modesty, grace and simplicity: a point of view which Faurence scornfully rejected. "Bah, this is owl's talk! Folk take you at your own appraisal of yourself; the skulking dog gets kicked, and rightly so!"

Miro Hetzel saw no need to pursue the subject. Faurence Dacre's views were not absolutely unreasonable, and, after all, school was often enough described as a social laboratory, or a world in miniature, where each person learned how to optimize his personality. But would Faurence Dacre learn? The esteem of one's fellows, especially at a place like Trembling Waters, could not be dragooned or commanded; Miro, in fact, was not at all sure whence it derived, or even if the subject deserved speculation.

Faurence and Miro both joined the chess club. In the

tournament Miro beat Faurence quite handily. When Miro said "checkmate," Faurence lifted his topaz eyes and stared at Miro a long slow minute. Then he raised his hand and for a moment Miro thought he planned to send the board spinning across the room. "Better luck next time," said Miro cheerfully.

"Chess is not a game of luck."

"Oh, I don't know. Sometimes a clever line of play can be spoiled by a stupid move of the adversary. Isn't that luck?"

"Yes. But I can't see that you made any stupid moves."

"I hope not. I played to win."

"I played to win too." The two strolled out across the compound. Faurence's face underwent a series of transparent changes: from perplexity through gloom to a grim frozen calm.

The two sprawled on the grass under the crooked branches of an upside-down tree. "So then," said Faurence, "you need only to beat Cloy Routhe for the championship."

Miro, chewing a grass stem, nodded impassively.

"I can't understand it," muttered Faurence. "This is not the way it should be."

Miro started to speak, then laughed: a small choked laugh of wonder and incredulity. "Really, you can't alter the way the world goes by sheer effort of will!"

"Here we differ," said Faurence, "though I put my philosophy in terms somewhat difficult to communicate. Essentially this: I must be best because I am best. The equation has imperatives working in two directions, and I adopt this as the basic premise of my being. X signifies and must signify Y; Y signifies and must signify X. The system, like any other, yields corollaries and vectors. The best is accorded what is best: he gains the power to realize his wishes, to embarrass his enemies, to use the advantages of wealth. When I am confronted by what seems a discrepancy in the equation, or a flaw, then I must make an adjustment or a clarification: not in the equation, which by the premise has unalterable force, but in the matching of terms to the variables of existence."

"Your premise may be faulty," observed Miro lazily. "Whereupon the whole system breaks down. After all, other persons form equations too."

Faurence gave his head a decisive shake. "I am convinced otherwise. The world is mine; I need only learn to use the equation. Today you won the chess game; impossible if I had worked the equation properly!"

Miro, amused by Faurence's ruminations, laughed again. "The only way to win a chess game is to play better chess. If we played a hundred games I would beat you ninety-five times, unless you altered your style. Do you know why? Because you play too boldly, and think to overwhelm the opponent through sheer élan."

Faurence said coldly, "Not true. I am the superior player, you cannot defeat me except by a fluke."

Miro shrugged. "Whatever you like. I care nothing for the word 'best.' My adversary is myself, not you."

Faurence said, "Very well then. You acknowledge my superiority."

"Of course not. Such judgements, if ever they are necessary, will be made by others. But the subject is absurd; let us discuss other things."

"No. The talk is not absurd. I can defeat you and I will prove it." Faurence brought out a pocket chess set and placed it on the grass. "Let us play another game. Choose." He held out his hands.

Miro looked at the board. Two black pawns were missing. Did Faurence hold a black piece in each of his hands? Miro took a white pawn and said: "This time you shall choose." He held out his hands.

After a moment Faurence touched one of the hands and discovered the white pawn, and so the game proceeded. As before Faurence played with burning concentration, topaz eyes luminous. Perhaps he had assimilated Miro's comments upon his style, for he played more cautiously, though he clearly chafed under the restrictions. Miro, hardly able to restrain his amusement, set a trap which he knew Faurence would be unable to resist; sure enough, Faurence thrust his rook far across the board, to corner Miro's bishop. Miro moved a pawn and the rook was pinned. Faurence studied the board, then yawned, and stretched. He looked across the compound. "There goes old Szantho for his weekly dip in the lake. What weird bathing dress he does affect!"

Miro glanced across the compound, then looked back to the board. Faurence's hand and wrist obscured his vision. Faurence moved a bishop. "Check," said Faurence. The rook was saved. Aha! thought Miro, the equation controls not only the cosmos, but also the rules of chess. He would not again remove his eyes from the board.

Two moves later, Miro saw opportunity for a bold sally of his own, directly through the territory guarded by the bishop before Faurence had diverted his attention. With a face totally devoid of expression, Miro moved his piece. Faurence protected; Miro moved again: "Check." Then, on his next move: "Checkmate."

Faurence carefully returned the board to his pocket. "Come," he said suddenly, "let us wrestle."

Miro shook his head. "The day is too warm for such exertion. And to what end? If I win, I wound your self-esteem. If you win, you reinforce your mysticism, which is not at all healthy for you."

"Still, wrestle you shall. Prepare yourself!" Faurence attacked, and Miro with a sigh of distaste was forced to defend himself. The two were much of a size, equally

CHAPTER 2

The capsule opened; Hetzel stepped out into an underground reception room, the floor tiled in white-blue arabesques. At one end water trickled from a gryphon's mouth into a wide bowl, with a formal landscape painted into the alcove behind. At the end opposite a door led into Dandyl Villa. A voice asked: "Who is calling, please?"

"Miro Hetzel."

A moment passed while Hetzel's image was scrutinized; then the voice said: "Welcome, please enter."

The door slid aside; Hetzel stepped forward, upon a plaque which raised him to ground level. Here Conwit Clent awaited him: a man an inch taller than Hetzel, and twenty pounds heavier, wearing a soft green suit and dark green sandals. His posture was not the best and his skin, as Hetzel had noted before, showed a dyspeptic gray undertone. Hetzel found it hard to recognize the brisk blond yachtsman of earlier years.

Clent's welcome was wholehearted. "I am obliged by your promptness, Xtl* Hetzel; I am relieved to see you."

*Xtl (pronounced "kstull"): the polite honorific in use on Cassander, ultimately derived from the word *stiletto* or "pirate captain."

"I only hope I can help you," said Hetzel. "Remember, as yet I don't even know what you want of me."

Clent uttered a strange feverish laugh. "I could tell you in one word—or rather two words—but you'd consider me insane. Let's go into the study. My wife is visiting friends and we shall not be disturbed." He led Hetzel along an airy hall hung with ferns and moth flowers into a room conceived in that charming style known as Archaic Lusitanian. He seated Hetzel in a chair of leather and wood, poured goblets of liquor, and settled himself on a couch. He gulped at his liquor, then leaned back with an air of grim resolve. "I first went to Dobor Effectuations and asked them to locate Faurence Dacre. They did their best, which was inadequate. While inquiring into Faurence Dacre's history, they discovered that you had been his classmate, and Xtl Dobor immediately recommended that I consult you. I believe he was annoyed that I had not fully confided in him."

"Rather more likely that he had no leads, or his men were all busy. What then is your problem?"

Clent spoke in a dead monotone. "I am a wealthy and socially prominent man. During my youth I occupied myself as you might expect: travel, sports, and I keep a fifty-foot ketch which I sail through the Shadow Islands, or sometimes out across the Florient to the Hesperids. For quite some years I remained a bachelor, although I enjoy female companionship well enough. I dallied here and there but never thought to marry until I met Perdhra Olruff at the home of a friend." Clent laughed ruefully. "I knew that I never wanted to be parted from her—an ambition I could not immediately fulfill, as she had come in the company of the brilliant and eminent surgeon Faurence Dacre, who was obviously enamoured of her.

"The next day we had lunch together. I asked if

Faurence Dacre meant anything to her, and she seemed, not evasive, but, let us say, reticent. To make a long story short, I learned that Dr. Dacre had intentions similar to my own, and that he had been wooing her with persistence and zeal. She could not help but take him seriously: he was, after all, distinguished and clever, and something of a celebrity as well. Nevertheless, for reasons best known to herself, Perdhra preferred me. Perhaps I seem easier to get along with. In due course we arranged to marry. Perdhra broke the news to Dr. Dacre as nicely as she could. He made appropriate remarks, and the matter seemed settled. The next day however he called me on the communicator, and issued a most amazing edit: I was to cease my attentions to Perdhra and never again approach her for the reason that he had chosen her for himself, which superseded all other considerations. When I could find my voice I told him to go to the devil. He merely remarked that this was my first, last, and only warning, that if I failed to obey his orders, I must face the consequences."

Clent paused, drank more liquor, and leaned back into the couch. "He frightened me. I admit it. I said nothing to Perdhra and naturally never considered giving her up. Instead, I suggested that we marry at once, here at Dandyl Villa, rather than at the Bargherac Temple as we had originally planned. Perdhra agreed; we invited a few relatives and close friends and were married. Immediately afterward we flew out to Port Sant, where I keep my ketch; we planned to cruise a month or two: to the Mirage Islands, then to Tinghal and, if the trade winds held, to Geraniol.

"We arrived at Port Sant. I found that the ketch had been broken into, and the direction sensor stolen. A trivial theft, really, and everything else seemed in order. I left Perdhra aboard and set off to the chandlery, a hundred yards along the shore.

"I never arrived. I don't know what happened to me. I recovered consciousness at the District Hospital, registered under a false name. And what of Perdhra! Neither kidnap nor threats nor fervent romance. She merely received a message that I had met with an accident, that the cruise must be postponed, and that I would communicate with her as soon as possible.

"I won't dwell on her reactions. Naturally she was bewildered. She returned to Cassander, and tried to discover what had happened to me with no success whatever.

"When I came alive I found that I had been unconscious for four days. I felt—strange. I can't describe the sensation exactly. But I knew that I had been tampered with." Clent's mouth twisted in a queer wry grin. "Well, there's no use beating around the bush. As soon as I returned to Dandyl Villa I took stock of myself, as well as I could, and discovered a scar along my scrotum. I called in a doctor at once. He examined me, and confirmed my suspicions. My seminal glands had been interfered with. The doctor performed a chromosomal analysis. The glands were transplants. The work had been done well; there was total continuity and no sign of rejection. I was Conwit Clent, true enough, but the male hormones were those of another man. The sperm was vital, but it was not my sperm; I could not father my own children. I knew of course who was responsible, but this had no bearing on my predicament. Who had contributed the glands? Where were my own?

"Either Faurence Dacre had implanted his own organs, which I seriously doubted, or glands regenerated from a small segment of his own organs, or organs from some detestable other source, which seemed most likely. And so there you have it." And Conwit Clent again displayed his sickly sheepish grin.

Hetzel tilted his goblet and watched the golden cusps

swing back and forth. "And what do you want me to do?"

"First—it goes without saying—I want back my missing parts. Perdhra and I both intend a family. This is impossible under present conditions. I might add that the idea of someone else's hormones draining into my system is indescribably repugnant.

"Secondly, I want Faurence Dacre punished. Legally or illegally, one way or another, I want him to regret his acts."

"Understandable," said Hetzel. "Does your wife know what has happened?"

Clent shook his head. "I can't bring myself to tell her. The doctor has explained that I have a peculiar heart condition which is not dangerous unless I exert myself and that I am taking medication to negate the possibllity of such exertion. She worries, but she remains cheerful and affectionate; I'm really most fortunate in my wife."

"Has Dacre communicated with either of you?"

"Not with me, and I don't believe with Perdhra."

"What did Dobor report?"

"Very little. Dacre cannot be located; according to his office he has gone off-planet for an indefinite period, which I gather is not unusual." Clent went to stand morosely by an arched window overlooking a garden court. Over his shoulder he said: "You can understand why I'm not concerned with expense." He turned around. "Will you take the case?"

"No question there," said Hetzel. "I'll take the case."

Clent muttered something under his breath and strode back to the couch, where he poured more liquor into both goblets.

Hetzel said, "You understand that I guarantee nothing. I can't even hold out much hope."

"I know. I realize all this."

"There is a condition you must agree to. You are a

strong-willed man, accustomed to doing as you please. But in a case like this, I can't work at cross-purposes with you."

"Understandable."

"I want complete control of the case. You must take no action without my approval. Otherwise there will be nothing but frustration for both of us."

Clent's agreement was perhaps a trifle glum. "I suppose this is reasonable enough. What of your fee?"

"I'll take a thousand SVU expense money now, for which I shall account to you. My fee will depend upon how much I achieve, what risks I take, how long I work. I can't name a specific figure at this moment."

Without a word Clent opened a cabinet, withdrew a packet of notes which he tossed to Hetzel. "One thousand SVI. No, I don't need a receipt."

CHAPTER 3

At the Hotel of the Worlds Hetzel communicated with Eban Dobor, senior partner of Dobor Investigations. "Ah, Hetzel," said the round affable face on the screen. "I'm not surprised to hear from you."

"I've just returned from Dandyl Villa. Thanks for the referral."

"Not at all. You were the obvious recommendation. It just doesn't smell like our kind of case."

"Thank you nonetheless. How did you learn about Trembling Waters?"

"We talked to Dacre's acquaintances, gathering biographical material for a surgical journal. He arrived at Cassander about two years ago, and so far as we can learn, he has no past—except for a casual mention of Trembling Waters Academy to a female companion. He speaks only in generalities, and evades questions with something like: 'aha! But that was then and this is now!' or 'Dull, stupid and trivial, every minute of it; let's talk of something else.' He's paid everyone off at his office except a receptionist; she almost certainly knows nothing."

"What of his professional license?"

"It tells us nothing. The municipality recognizes no diplomas or accreditations; standards vary too widely

167

across the Reach. The Cassander Medical Board gives a
ten-day examination and issues licenses only on this
basis. Scores are a matter of public record. Faurence
Dacre achieved a rating of 98.2 in a possible 100, which
is almost unheard of. The clerk of the Medical Board
gave me a funny grin and a shake of the head when we
discussed that rating. I asked 'Does anyone ever cheat?'
He said: 'You'd be astounded at the boldness, these men
we're supposed to trust!'

" 'And this score of 98.2?'

" 'It's not my place to say a word. If a candidate con-
vinces the Medical Board, who am I to cast him out?
He's a clever one, I'll say that, is Dr. Dacre.'

"So draw your own conclusions. He wasn't popular
with his colleagues, though they won't say why. A bit of
envy, no doubt, because Dacre went straight to the top."

"Any love affairs?"

"All over the place, but nothing serious until he met
Perdhra Olruff. Then the two were seen everywhere: a
most eye-catching pair, according to reports."

"Where did he go after he left Trembling Waters?"

"No information. I tried the Trembling Waters alumni records. 'All information is secret and held in sacred
trust!'—that's what old Dominie Cheasling told me.
They're afraid of outside trouble; lots of rich folk send
their boys here. I was allowed to look into the yearbook.
Faurence Dacre's out-of-school address was Caelzie
Empire Inn, here in Cassander. Useless information;
they keep records only three years, and no one remem-
bers him or his family. There are no Dacres on Thesse.
That's the file and it's all in your lap."

"I'll have to start from where you left off."

"Indeed. And where will that be?"

"Back at Trembling Waters."

CHAPTER 4

Years had come and gone; lives launched in hope and innocence had lost momentum or gone awry; but Trembling Waters Academy had altered little if any. Hetzel noted a new boathouse alongside Tanjaree Cove; the upside-down trees sprawled across greater areas; the greenstone offices, laboratories, classrooms, workshops, and dormitories seemed a trifle smaller, somewhat drowsier and dustier under the enormous Palladian elms imported from far Dashbourne Planet, where, four hundred years before, Dominie Kasus, founder of Trembling Waters Academy, had first seen the light of day. Otherwise all was as Hetzel remembered. He landed his rented air car on the visitor's plat, alighted, and sauntered toward Kasus Hall.

The time was middle afternoon, too early for his purposes. He seated himself on a bench beside the quadrangle and watched the activity, which no matter how similar in form to that of twenty years before, seemed different in kind. How open, how morning-fresh these young faces! Hetzel found remarkable the idea that he himself had been one of this uninformed group. Not a sentimental man, he nevertheless felt a seep of melancholy . . . A gong. Hetzel glanced at his watch. The administrative officers, if routines went as before—and why should they not!—would now be departing their cubicles and Kasus Hall would be left to the care of either Cholly the janitor, or his successor, or his successor's successor.

Hetzel waited another half hour then strolled across the quadrangle to Kasus Hall. He mounted the steps and entered the vestibule, which smelled exactly as before. To his left was a large chamber, known as the Registrar's Office, which also served a variety of miscellaneous functions. Here, as he had expected, Hetzel found Cholly the janitor; a few degrees more stooped, a trifle more convex of paunch, lacking half his proud ruff of hair, but essentially as before. Certain institutions verged on permanency, thought Hetzel.

Cholly looked up from his work. "Sorry, sir, offices are closed for the day."

"What a nuisance!" declared Hetzel. "I have flown out from Cassander for nothing!"

"Sorry, sir. For something urgent you could roust out Dominie Cheasling, though he wouldn't thank you."

Hetzel appeared to cogitate. "Perhaps that won't be necessary, if you could lend a hand. I'd pay for any inconvenience, of course, and we wouldn't need to bother Dominie Cheasling."

Cholly spoke in a careful voice: "What is it that you want, sir?"

"I am an attorney-at-law, and I am trying to locate one of the school alumni so that I can pay over an inheritance. For this I need his address, which should be in the files yonder."

Cholly laughed sourly. "Not a chance, sir. Dominie Cheasling doesn't allow that sort of thing. We've got too many rich men's sons here, and there's always fear of a kidnapping or something of the like."

"From the out-of-date files?" scoffed Hetzel. "Hardly likely."

"You don't know Dominie Cheasling, sir. He doesn't do things halfway." Cholly clearly made no connection between ex-student Miro Hetzel and this gray-eyed man with the soft black hair.

Hetzel brought forth his billfold and tapped it thoughtfully upon the counter. "In that case, it's lucky that I arrived late." He withdrew a five-SVU note. "Perhaps you will allow me to step over yonder and discover my information. We need not trouble Dominie Cheasling at all."

Cholly eyed the note with a curled lip. "How do you know the information is over yonder?"

"Where else would it be?"

"Mmf. Dominie Cheasling would have my skin . . ." he glanced sidelong at the note. "Can you make that 10 SVU?"

"Rather than waste my trip out here, yes." Hetzel produced another five SVU.

"Wait then," said Cholly, with sudden alacrity. "I want to lock the front door and hang on the chain; then no one can surprise us."

Returning, Cholly made a conspiratorial sign. "No matter what, my name must never be mentioned."

"This I guarantee," said Hetzel, and Cholly allowed him behind the counter. Hetzel went directly to the "admissions" file, and pulling open a drawer, found the plaque for his last year at Trembling Waters.

"You are deft with those files," observed Cholly in a skeptical voice. "How do you work with such certainty?"

"Institutions are much alike," said Hetzel absently. "Now let me see—ah yes; the repro." He inserted the plaque and read the index which flashed on the screen. Cholly came to crane his neck, but Hetzel warned him back. "The less you know the better, in case Dominie Cheasling's suspicions ever are aroused."

Cholly moved fretfully away. "Hurry then; I can't delay all evening."

Hetzel adjusted the indices. As Eban Dobor had reported, Faurence Dacre had stated his local address to be the Caelzie Empire Inn, in Cassander. Hetzel ignored the registration card and focused upon Dacre's original application for admittance.

"Someone is coming up the steps!" grumbled Cholly. "You can stay no longer!"

"A moment," said Hetzel. With his stylus he wrote an address:

> *Gandardie House, Willanella,*
> *Disten; Derd Province, Semblat*
> *Wittenmond*

And below he wrote a name, the signature on the application:

> *Vela, Lady Keurboom*

CHAPTER 5

Hetzel reported to Clent, and without preliminaries said: "I suspect that Dacre has gone off-planet."

"Why do you say that?" asked Clent. The comfort he had derived from Hetzel's participation in the case had worn off; he now seemed as morose and woebegone as ever.

"The accretion of several ideas, none in themselves decisive. In Cassander your marriage has made him look a fool, or so he believes. I suspect that Cassander has lost all charm for him. He also knows that you are looking for him, though I doubt if he is seriously alarmed; you are now nothing to him except a figure of contempt."

Clent made a husky sound deep in his throat.

"Further, it seems to be his habit to travel off-world at frequent intervals, which suggests that he maintains another residence, or headquarters, though this of course is not necessarily true. Still, when one takes all with all, there seems reason to believe that he has departed Thesse. That at least is my guess."

"But where?" asked Clent in a hollow voice. "Twenty ships leave Cassander every day; there are a hundred worlds in every direction. To go out to find a man is like trying to find a drop of water in the ocean!"

"In a certain sense, this is true," Hetzel agreed. "Still no one moves without leaving traces. The ordinary method is to go down to the space port and try to discover on which ship he departed: obviously a near-hopeless job if a person has tried to conceal his movements.

"The alternate system is to start in the past, before he needed subterfuge, and discover the places he favored, to which he might be apt to return, and this is the method I propose to use."

"I fear that you have left me behind," growled Clent.

"We can either trace his life backward, or trace him forward," Hetzel explained. "Going back, I have no clues, no indications whatever. Going forward I have at least one clue: the name and address of his mother."

Clent was genuinely startled. "Where did you get that?"

Like the professional magician, Hetzel preferred to conceal his methods, in order that his effects might the better be appreciated. He said politely, "I make it a rule never to reveal the sources of my information. You will understand the reason for this."

Clent, who understood nothing of the sort, said blankly: "Yes, naturally."

"I personally will go to Wittenmond to interview Dacre's mother," said Hetzel. "Still we will not neglect the obvious. Another man will try to trace Dacre's movements from Cassander, although I doubt if he will have any more luck than Eban Dobor."

Clent spoke in a glum voice: "When will I hear from you?"

"As well as I can I'll keep you abreast of events, but don't expect news until I call."

Clent grunted. "If you run out of money, call for more. All I want is—well—results."

"I'll do my best."

CHAPTER 6

Around that enormous yellow blaze known as Jingkens Star swung several dozen planets, all of which had been surveyed by Gieter Jingkens, a jovial freebooter of the Great Expansions. Three of these, the so-called Sister Planets, were alike in size, mass, density, atmosphere, climate and land-water ratios; their flora and fauna had elaborated to approximately the same degree. These special conditions had not escaped the attention of Gaean scientists; the correspondences, analogies, and divergences had proved material for ten thousand monographs and a whole new evolutionary chronometry had been established on the basis of the so-called "Jingkens parallelisms."

The "Sister Planets," Wittenmond, Gietersmond, and Skalkemond, originally had been settled by three epodes of the Reformed Anti-Gnomic Credentists; and the disparate development of these people was of no great interest to social anthropologists. The folk of Wittenmond had created a thriving mercantile system, and traded throughout the System. Consciously, or unconsciously, they extended the concept of exact measurement and specified quality to the most ordinary details of daily life. Every gradation of luxury was labeled and value rated; prerogatives, recreation, property, garments, and adjuncts—all must appropriately be matched to status. Music, architecture, cuisine, even gardening and horticulture: all were arranged in hierarchies of taste and suitability. The society, necessarily stratified into an elaborate aristocracy, was by no means frozen, and movement across the castes preoccupied the thoughts of every Witt. Far from incurring resentment, the situation was universally supported, inasmuch as the gradated society, rather than alienating or isolating folk into solopsistic cells, made each person intensely aware of his fellows; each Witt, no matter how menial or how exalted, if nothing else relished his participation in the complicated game, and took pride in mastering the elaborate rules. The sophisticated Witt, if taken to task for the inequities of life on Wittenmond, merely pointed out that the same inequities existed everywhere, but that on Wittenmond they were acknowledged and codified.

Folk from other worlds were wont to marvel at the multifarious details which seemed to clutter the existence of the Witts, not appreciating that the codes precisely stipulated the Witt way of life; that their own seemingly spare society entailed a far greater intricacy, owing to ambiguities, allusions, implications, flexible sets of moods and overtones, symbols which might or might not signify, superiorities and inferiorities enforced by subtle little contests which created far more frustration than the impersonal distinctions of the Witts; and in the end each society seemed to the other an impenetrable murk.

Arriving at Diestl on Wittenmond, Hetzel discovered a city of considerable charm, built in a series of levels on the hills surrounding Mount Flouderklaf. The Lemon River swinging down from the northern plains passed through the industrial district, then angled away to the Irruptor Ocean, twenty miles distant across a rolling landscape of forests and gardens and manorial estates of high-bred merchant princes.

The space port occupied a square mile of inordinately valuable real estate only a quarter mile north of the Diestl financial district; the commerciants of the Diestl well understood the value of convenience.

From the space port Hetzel rode a slideway to the Traveler's Hotel, his policy being to assure himself of comfortable lodging before all else. In his pleasant if sterile room he consulted the Directory and learned that Diestl was divided into seventy-three purlieus, each with its particular set of characteristics, which the directory faithfully noted. Hetzel thus discovered Willanella to be a district of middle-nobility residences, each situated on a plot of no less than 1.2 acres, valued at no less than SVU* two hundred thousand, and maintained by at least six servants. The Directory also assured him that Vela, Lady Keurboom, still occupied Gangardie House in Willanella, and listed her address, the members of her household, which included herself; Lazar, Lord Keurboom; a butler, a cook, a head gardener, and six underservants, with a communication code for each. No person who might have been Faurence Dacre appeared on the list.

Hetzel, lacking any definite plan of procedure, hired a flitter which whisked him westward to Willanella and deposited him on a terrace fifty yards from Gangardie House.

By moving only twenty yards and climbing an embankment Hetzel was afforded an excellent view of that structure which presumably had nurtured Faurence Dacre during his childhood. Hetzel put a pair of macroid spectacles to his eyes, and studied the ornate façade, but learned nothing of consequence. . . . A movement attracted his eye. From the back garden came a dark-haired woman, wearing a white frock which swept the turf as she walked. She was tall and imposing rather than portly, although her face bulged at cheek, jowl, and under the chin. Still, her eyes flashed grandly, and the angles of her face hinted of an exotic

*SVU: Standard Value Unit; the worth of one standard man's unskilled labor under standard conditions for a period of one Gaean hour; the single and only commodity of unalterable value.

beauty now unhappily departed.

Hetzel watched her as with great fervor she cut a bouquet of flowers. With what enthusiasm did she seize upon a choice bloom! With what repugnance did she spurn the overblown blossom! With what raptures of indignation did she stamp her white slipper upon a noxious insect!

Hetzel removed his spectacles. The woman was excitable and emotional; to approach her directly would surely arouse her suspicions.

Hetzel descended the embankment and sauntered past Gangardie House. He paused beside a residence across the way, where an elderly man in old clothes pruned a rose tree. Hetzel paused to watch the elderly man's techniques. He remarked upon the density of the hedge, the fragrance of the flowers, and a conversation was underway. Hetzel identified himself as a wealthy nobleman of Old Earth who might be interested in buying a house.

"Unlikely to be anything here in Willanella," his acquaintance remarked. "We're all pretty well established."

"That may be," said Hetzel. "However I was told of a noble mansion which might go on the market soon. I wonder if it could be that one yonder, across the way."

"Hoho! Gangardie House? No chance whatever. That's the Keurboom place; they've been there forever."

" 'Keurboom' you say? I know that name. Don't they have a famous son—a scientist or a surgeon or something of the like?"

"Leave Sir Lazar out of it. That would be Lady Keurboom's boy by her first spouse. I've heard that he's finally made a success of himself, but only after leaving home, since he never got along with Sir Lazar."

"Not unusual in such a situation. Does he never attempt a reconciliation with the old man?"

"Not to my knowledge. I haven't seen him for years."

CHAPTER 7

Hetzel, making inquiries here and there about Diestl, learned that the Keurboom family originally had prospered in the publishing business, and that Lazar Lord Keurboom now lived on the proceeds of investments. His first wife had borne him no children; after a divorce Sir Lazar had espoused a foreign woman, a certain Vela Woxonoy from Todnie, who came to Diestl in a theatrical company, accompanied by her young son. Keurboom, now a semi-invalid, divided his time between his home and his club. Hetzel decided that the optimum occasion to seek a meeting with Sir Lazar would be at his club, where refusal to confer with a foreign gentleman, perhaps a customer, might be considered eccentric.

Accordingly, Hetzel stepped into the Apollonian Club at an appropriate hour and dispatched a message requesting a few moments of Lord Keurboom's time.

Lord Keurboom made him wait ten minutes, then stumped gracelessly into the small sitting room where Hetzel waited. He inspected Hetzel from the doorway: a stout heavy-legged man of no great stature with a pale complexion, scant sandy hair, and a massive prognathous jaw curiously at odds with the remainder of his rather bland countenance. "Well sir?" he demanded in a rasping voice. "You are Miro Hetzel?"

"Correct, Sir Lazar."

"And what do you wish to talk to me about?"

"I won't waste your time or my own, sir. I want to learn the present whereabouts of your stepson Faurence Dacre."

Keurboom's rasp became a sibilant whistle; Hetzel wondered if he might not be talking through a synthevox. "Do not speak to me of that person. I have nothing to say."

Hetzel nodded with understanding. "Then you have no kind recollections of Dr. Dacre."

"Dr. Dacre, pah!" Keurboom's lips worked; wetness showed at the corners of his mouth. He struggled for words and managed to say: "That is all, sir. I will say no more!"

Hetzel held up his finger. "Let me define my interest. Faurence Dacre has committed flagrant irregularities at Cassander on Thesse. I want to find him so that he may be brought to account. We talk in complete confidence, I assure you this; your name will never be mentioned."

Keurboom slowly sank into a seat. "I do not know where he is. If I did . . ."

"But perhaps you can tell me other things, by which I can trace him. For instance—"

Keurboom held up his hand. "It all must be confidential, is that understood? No one must know, and this includes Lady Vela."

"I agree to your condition."

"Well then; what is important to you?"

"Whatever you can tell me."

Keurboom told a rambling tale, punctuated by spasms of fury which rendered his speech barely intelligible. "I tried to do my best for the boy. It was clear that his mother spoiled him and filled his mind with

nonsense. Despite her lamentations I sent him away to a
fine school on Thesse; the Trembling Waters Academy.
Well, he lasted a term or two and then they sent him
home, to the joy of his mother, and we had him around
the house once more. For a time he kept quiet; he was
reading mysticism: rot and stupid nonsense! His mother
ordered me not to bother him, that he was preparing for
a career in psychology. Then for a time I didn't see him
at his books and I began to wonder. I found him in the
potting shed—his 'laboratory,' he called it. He was
performing experiments, right enough, upon the
gardener's daughter! He had hypnotized her, dosed her
with vile drugs, and played her all manner of weird
tricks. I caught him red-handed at the business and
turned him out of the house. His mother was horrified,
and made excuses, but for once I had my way, and
Faurence was sent packing. I washed my hands of him.
For a month or two he lived with his aunt, then his
mother put him into the Technical Institute at
Narghuys, on Gietersmond. Naturally I was required to
foot the bills. I understand that he undertook the medical program and it seems that he accomplished a
brilliant success. His mother will not mention him to me
and I believe that she is trying to put him out of her
mind." Sir Lazar made a curt gesture. "That is all I can
tell you of Faurence Dacre, as he calls himself."

"Should he not call himself Faurence Dacre?"

"The question is one of principle. My wife and her
first spouse were united informally. Witt law stipulates
the mother's name for the yield of such unions.
Faurence has flouted this law, ignoring the wishes of his
mother; he rejects both 'Keurboom' and 'Woxonoy' in
favor of the name carried by his footloose father . . ."

CHAPTER 8

Two hours after his interview with Lord Keurboom, Hetzel boarded the passenger ship *Sobranad,* bound for Gietersmond. Arriving at Narghuys in the middle of the night, he went directly to the Cosmolux Hotel across Prater Huss Square. After assuring himself of accommodation he returned to the square and went to an outdoor cafe, half-concealed by the wares of all-night flower vendors. The waiter brought him a carafe of local wine and a sizzling dish of sausages. At times, thought Hetzel, the perquisites of his occupation were notably agreeable. Gietersmond was to be preferred to Wittenmond, so he decided. The air seemed more bracing; the skies spread with a farther, wider, higher arch; the winds blew (so it seemed) with less constraint. Hetzel wondered about the composition of the two atmospheres. A higher concentration of oxygen? A different mix of inert gases? More or less carbon dioxide, or ozone, or nitrous oxide, or gases more rare and dilute? Such variations produced subtle psychological displacements, which across the years would accumulate.

A people's soul was pictured in its architecture: such was the aphorism of the ancient sage Unspiek, Baron Bodissey. To Hetzel's mind it carried conviction. The structures of Narghuys could never be considered austere, or simple, or spare; still they seemed less elaborate than those of Diestl. The Witts emphasized intricacy at the expense of integration. No curve related to any other curve; variousness held precedence over unity; no texture was repeated if human ingenuity could conceive another.

The folk of Narghuys, using a similar battery of motifs, achieved a surprisingly different effect. The structures of Narghuys displayed less idiosyncracy and more style; curves were less opulent, and a logical correlation frequently united the various parts and aspects of a building. The differences in architecture mirrored the different preoccupations of the people. The Witts traded; the Giets engineered, designed, crafted. The Witts sold goods; the Giets sold expertise. The Giet technical academies were famous across the Reach; the Giet shops and laboratories produced a constant stream of innovative products, not necessarily all of practical value, which the Witts were glad to sell.*

Immediately after breakfast Hetzel took himself to the Narghuys Academy of Medical Sciences. A direct approach, so he had found, sometimes yielded as much information as a week's subterfuge. He went directly to the Information Counter and addressed himself to the clerk: a personable young woman in dark blue and white uniform.

---

*On Skalkemond, the third and outermost of the so-called "Sister Planets," were situated the great banks, financial institutions, academies of mathematics, cosmology, projective speculation, and esthetics, conservatories of music theory and critical evaluation. In comparison with the architecture of its sister worlds that of Skalkemond seemed spare and severe.

The Skalks, more intensively preoccupied with abstraction than either the Witts or Giets, suffered a wider and deeper range of mental disturbances. They were especially concerned with physical security and had developed an amazing system of area control which reduced crime and violence to a minimum.

"I am interested in the career of Dr. Faurence Dacre, who trained here," said Hetzel. "Who could I consult in this regard? Conceivably you?"

The clerk smiled; Hetzel's admiration seemed to cause her no distress. "How is the name spelled?" Receiving the information she touched buttons and dials, but the screen remained blank. She shook her head. "No references. Other folk also have inquired, so I see."

"Perhaps he used the name Woxonoy—Faurence Woxonoy."

" 'Faurence Woxonoy'?" She busied herself with the screen. "He studied here for eight years: until twelve years ago, actually."

"And then where did he go?"

"I don't know, sir; the information isn't here. You had best make inquiries of his old provost."

"Very well; who would that be?"

The clerk checked the record. "Dr. Aartemus. I'm afraid that he is occupied until this afternoon."

"Perhaps you will make an appointment for me. My name is Miro Hetzel."

"Certainly, sir. Shall I say in connection with Dr. Faurence Woxonoy?"

"If you like."

At the appointed hour Hetzel entered the chambers of Dr. Aartemus, to discover a thin gray man, rather small, with a pale broad forehead under a coarse gray stubble of hair. His expression, so it seemed to Hetzel, was at once sagacious, tolerant and sardonic; when he stood up, Hetzel saw that he was lame. " 'Physician, heal thyself!' " intoned Dr. Aartemus. "Luckily the physician of today can heed the injunction—if he chooses. I do not so choose. I am supported by tireless metal which never causes inconvenience. I fear neither fallen arches, ingrown toenails, itch, callus, chafe, scale, or any of a thousand disturbances. I am not a selfish man; if you like I will on this instant amputate your own legs."

Hetzel smilingly shook his head. "I am not the faddist you apparently believe me to be."

"As you wish. I believe that you have a question to put to me?"

"True, in connection with a certain Faurence Woxonoy, who now calls himself Dr. Faurence Dacre. I am anxious to locate him."

"You are not alone," said Dr. Aartemus. "Over the years I have had several similar inquiries." He leaned back in his chair. "Normally our rules are rigid; we tend to discretion, if for no other reason than self-protection. We never recommend any of our graduates, although we cheerfully provide information as to those who have failed their courses. The case of Faurence Woxonoy, or Dacre, if you prefer, is different. He was a brilliant student with a genuinely innovative mind; still, he failed certain of his courses and was not graduated."

"Indeed! But he practices medicine without a qualm. Is this proper?"

"It is realistic. The Gaean Reach comprises countless communities; each must apply its own standards. A graduate of Podmarsh School of Medicine at Sek Sek on Wicker would not be allowed to treat a case of hiccups here on Gietersmond. On the other hand, though Faurence Dacre failed here at Narghuys, he went forth superbly equipped to practice anywhere across the Reach."

"In that case, why was he not graduated?"

"To state the matter succinctly, he cheated. I—better to say, we—discredited him for deficiencies of the personality rather than those of technique. He had no need to cheat. He merely took exception to certain of my remarks and set himself to demonstrate that he could achieve honors in my class without performing any of my assignments. I watched him the whole of the term; after all, I am not a supid man. I bided my time, because I recognized that a small setback, a small reprimand, would make no impression on him. All term he falsified his work, by a variety of ingenious means. I was more experienced and more ingenious. On the last day I spoke to the class, which incidentally was a very good class; I had been forced to send only five persons down for further work. 'I congratulate you,' I told them. 'All have done excellent work. Except one. That one is Faurence Woxonoy who, for reasons best known to himself, has cheated consistently throughout the term.' I now exhibited on the demonstration screen the various incidents which I had recorded. The class of course was greatly amused. Halfway through my demonstration Woxonoy rose to his feet and left the room.''

Hetzel grunted. "After that what happened to him?"

"I have no sure knowledge. I heard that he had gone to work in the Southern Torpeltines, at a place called Masmodo." Dr. Aartemus spoke into a mesh. "Who has the practice at Masmodo, on Jamus Amaha?"

A voice came back. "Dr. Leuvil, now retired. The nearest active practitioner would be at Kroust."

"Thank you." Dr. Aartemus returned to Hetzel. "Jamus Amaha is the wildest area of the planet—only half-civilized, really."

Hetzel reflected a moment. "Perhaps, sir, you would do me the favor of calling Dr. Leuvil, to inquire after Dr. Dacre."

Dr. Aartemus raised his eyes to the ceiling, then shrugged. He worked buttons on his communicator but elicited only a set of fretful buzzing sounds. A woman at last appeared on the screen. "Masmodo operator."

"I am trying to raise Dr. Leuvil," said Aartemus. "I have had no success whatever."

"Dr. Leuvil is retired; he no longer answers the communicator. Try Dr. Winke on Doubtful Island."

"One moment. Can you get a message to Dr. Leuvil? Please notify him that Dr. Aartemus at Narghuys is waiting to speak to him."

The operator grudgingly acknowledged that such a process was possible. "Just a moment, if you please."

Five minutes later the screen crackled and flared; amidst slowly expanding sets of green halations appeared the face of a blond young woman in a limp nurse's uniform. Her face was round and peevishly pretty, if somewhat fleshy. "Who is calling? Doctor who?"

"Dr. Aartemus, of Narghuys Medical Sciences. I'd like a word with Dr. Leuvil."

"Is he expecting a call from you?"

"I think not; however—"

"You are an old friend?"

"I think not; however—"

"Then Dr. Leuvil will not speak with you."

"Surely this is most surly of him! I am a colleague—neither a bill collector nor a charity patient!"

"I'm sorry, Doctor. My orders have been made very clear to me."

"Very well then. Please ask Dr. Leuvil if he knows the whereabouts of Dr. Faurence Dacre, or Dr. Faurence Woxonoy, as he might have called himself?"

The nurse gave a mincing little laugh. "I am certain that he will discuss Dr. Dacre with neither you nor anyone else."

"Do you yourself know Dr. Dacre?"

"Yes indeed."

"Can you tell me where he is now?"

The nurse shook her head. "I couldn't even guess."

"I thank you for your assistance." Dr. Aartemus dulled his screen, swung around toward Hetzel. "So there you have it. I can do no more."

"Dr. Aartemus, I am most grateful to you."

CHAPTER 9

To travel from Narghuys to Masmodo on Jamus Amaha entailed far more difficulty than the journey from Diestl to Narghuys. Hetzel rode south by airship to Jonder at the head of the Great Fish River, he then boarded a local connector which stopped at every small community along the Malabar Littoril, and which finally discharged him at Cape Jaun, and thence to Paunt on Kletterer Island by ocean skimmer.

Away to the west, over the horizon and far beyond, extended the Torpeltines, a series of rocky hulks and spires, each surrounded by a fringe of beach and a few hundred yards of gangee, sprugge, magenta tea, cardenil bush, and coconut palms, these latter imported by an unknown number of stages from Old Earth. Few of the Torpeltines were inhabited by man. About half had been declared reserves for the indigenous Flamboyards; others lacked all inducement to human presence, since the sea harbored sea scrags, war eel, shatterbone and antler fish, while raptap, sword fly, corkscrew ticks, and saltators infested the beaches.

At Paunt, Hetzel rented an air car and flew five hundred miles down the chain of Torpeltines to Jamus Amaha. Masmodo, the principal settlement of the island, included a hotel, three taverns, several stores and warehouses, a small hospital or dispensary, several official offices, a boatyard, and a number of scattered residences. Rickety docks extended into the harbor, angling and dog-legging; to these docks were moored fishing boats. Enormous black sneezewood trees shaded the streets and lined the waterfront.

Hetzel landed his airboat behind the post office and secured lodging at the Great Western Hotel. The time was early afternoon. Jingkens Star, halfway down the blue-purple sky, glared on the sand streets, extracted a rank resinous odor from the paper-thin sneezewood shags, gleamed and flickered along the sluggish swells which eased under the docks.

From the verandah of the hotel Hetzel surveyed the long main thoroughfare: from the waterfront past the municipal offices facing the hotel, up the slope to the dispensary and Dr. Leuvil's cottage nearby.

After ten minutes of reflection Hetzel walked down to the docks. A few men tinkered with their fishing gear; others squatted on short crooked legs, looking out across the harbor. An unlovely lot, thought Hetzel: squat and dumpy with narrow foreheads, heavy chins and jaws, protruding noses, pendulous ears. These were Arsh, whose forbears, escaping the Corrective Institute on Sanctissimus Island, had taken refuge in the Jamus Amaha jungles. After centuries of isolation the Arsh had become a small but definite racial singularity.*

Hetzel walked out along one of the creaking docks, to Dongg's Tavern at the seaward end. The interior was cool and capacious; the waterwood canes of which the

*The legendary starmenter Yane Cargus contracted with the all-male fugitives. He agreed to deliver one hundred young females for a fee of five hundred red sarcenels, the sarcenel being a jewellike object taken from a Flamboyard's sensorium. Cargus raided the Convent of the Divine Prism at Blenny, on Lutus, capturing two hundred and thirty novitiates. Upon delivering his cargo, he required a thousand sarcenels or nothing, emphasizing the volume discount. The fugitives in their turn pointed out that sarcenels were rare, that the Flam-

walls were woven allowed a filigree of Jingkens's light to sift across the plank floors. Three Arsh, wearing only loose crotch wraps and curl-brimmed hats with tall concave-conical peaks, crouched together drinking beer from huge pots. They swung slantwise glances over their shoulders, which somehow seemed like sneers; then they turned and continued their guttural conversation.

Hetzel took a seat and the barmaid presently came forward: a young blond woman, large hipped and well fleshed, her face not so much hard as impervious.

"Sir, what's your wish?"

"Something cool and easy. What would you suggest?"

"We make a nice punch, with rum, cabinche, tartlip juice, and lemon squash."

"Exactly right."

With stately mien the barmaid served a greenish yellow mixture which Hetzel found pleasantly astringent. "Very nice," he told the barmaid.

She returned a frigid nod. Her face was round, like Dr. Leuvil's nurse; not too long ago she might also have been pretty.

Hetzel asked: "Is the weather always this warm at Masmodo?"

"Most of the year, except during rains."

The nurse, Hetzel decided, was definitely more attractive than the barmaid, whose billows were perilously close to sheer fat, even allowing for the difference of perhaps five years in age. "Are you a native of these parts?" he asked.

---

boyards ferociously resisted attack, that, for eighty-six men, two hundred and thirty females were redundant by more than a factor of two, and, most importantly, that the females were members of that ill-favored and swarthy race known as Gettucks: not at all what the fugitives had in mind. In the ensuing fight, Yane Cargus took thirty-four wounds from the sneezewood lances, but miraculously survived. The fugitives acquired two hundred and thirty females free of charge, and the Arsh race came into existence.

The barmaid merely gave him a sour smirk, and turned away to serve another customer. Hetzel meditatively consumed the punch, then, choosing his time, ordered a second of the same. "And have one yourself."

"Thanks, I don't drink."

In due course the rum punch was served. Hetzel asked: "What's to be done around here for amusement?"

"Sit here, drink, listen to the waves. Sometimes the Arsh tell nasty stories or kill each other. That's about the lot."

"At least if you get sick there's a hospital handy. Who's the doctor?"

"Doctor's retired; he won't take cases anymore."

"Oh? I thought I saw a nurse go into the cottage. She looked just a bit like you."

" 'Nurse'?" The barmaid raised her near-invisible eyebrows at Hetzel's lack of perception. "She just takes care of things. Nurses her father, I suppose you'd say. Do you really think she looks like me?" The last was a scornful challenge.

"Not really, except that she's blonde. You've got character and style, if you don't mind my saying so."

"Hmf. I'm wasting it here."

"Why not have a drink?"

"I can't touch the stuff; I come all over blotches."

"We can't have that!" said Hetzel with fulsome emphasis. "By the way, when I looked in the Masmodo directory, I noticed the name of another doctor. It might have been an old directory." Hetzel glanced at the barmaid questioningly.

"Likely it was." She turned away.

Hetzel returned to the hotel verandah, put on his macrospectacles and sat watching the hospital. Halfway through the afternoon the "nurse"—if such she were— stepped out upon the verandah to confer with the driver of a grocer's wagon. Half an hour later a stooped man came slowly out upon an upper terrace and seated himself in the shade of an umbrella. Under a curl-brimmed tail-peaked Arsh hat Hetzel saw damp locks of gray hair, a pallid complexion, a long drooping nose. Once he looked directly into a pair of milky gray eyes. Dr. Leuvil —if this were he—peered this way and that across the landscape. Hetzel suspected that his eyesight was not entirely keen.

Hetzel removed his macrospectacles, stepped down from the verandah, and ambled up toward the doctor's cottage. The doctor either would or would not see him; there was no particular reason for subtlety or delay.

The doctor would not see Hetzel. Upon Hetzel's approach the doctor rose to his feet, shook his head in displeasure, and groped his way back into the cottage. When Hetzel rang the doorbell a small panel opened and the nurse looked out. "Doctor Leuvil is retired. He no longer takes patients."

"I am not a patient," said Hetzel. "I want only a few facts in regard to his former associate, Dr. Dacre."

"Dr. Leuvil will see no one, sir."

"Just take him the message. I will wait."

The nurse closed the panel and presently returned. "He does not wish to discuss Dr. Dacre."

"Tell him that Dr. Dacre has got himself into trouble and that his information may have an important bearing upon the matter."

The nurse shook her head and her blond corkscrew ringlets bobbed and bounced. "I won't tell him because the message would only upset him. He definitely will not discuss Dr. Dacre; it would make him sick." She started to close the panel; Hetzel held it open. "Really; is he in all that bad condition?"

The nurse suddenly smiled; dimples appeared in her round face. Hetzel thought her quite charming. "He thinks he is; isn't that the same thing after all?"

"I don't know," said Hetzel. "Please give him my message and ask him to think it over. I will come back tomorrow."

"You need not bother." The panel closed.

Odd, thought Hetzel. He returned to the hotel, and from the verandah watched Jingkens Star settle into the Mondial Ocean.

Lights went on in the hotel restaurant; Hetzel went in for his evening meal. The waitress was frankly overweight. Her skin was pale; a profusion of blonde curls hung over her massive shoulders. Her cheeks were round; her bosom bulged, her haunches distended the cerise fabric of her pantaloons; all quivered and surged as she moved about her duties. Where the barmaid at Dongg's Tavern displayed a hard and bitter cynicism and the nurse at Dr. Leuvil's cottage a chilly aloofness, the waitress seemed affable and uncalculating. She advised Hetzel in regard to the sparse menu and suggested that instead of the mousy beer he test the more palatable sublume cider, whose potency was not to be despised. When Hetzel suggested that she herself take a quart of the cider, or whatever she preferred, she agreed upon the instant. Five minutes later, when the last diner had been served, she settled herself with a grunt of comfort into a chair beside Hetzel and drank down the cider with zest. Hetzel immediately called for two more quarts. "You drink with rare appreciation," said Hetzel. "It is a trait of which I approve."

The waitress turned her head toward the kitchen. "Freitzke! Freshen the tables! I am talking business with this gentleman!"

An adolescent girl, blond and already overendowed with feminine attributes, sullenly began to order the restaurant.

"Your sister?" asked Hetzel.

"She is my sister indeed. Look at the little fool; will

she never learn? Freitzke, serve from the right, clear from the left!"

"What difference does it make?" grumbled Freitzke. "There is no one at the tables."

"You must practice; how else will you learn?" The waitress turned back to Hetzel. "Poor Freitzke! We are a left-handed family: father, mother—now dead alas!— and all the girls, but Freitzke also thinks with her left hand. Nonetheless a dear good person, if inclined to fits of unreasonable sulking."

"The barmaid at Dongg's is also related?"

"Another sister."

"Then there is Dr. Leuvil's housekeeper, or would she be his nurse?"

"That scheming minx! She also is a sister. It is like mathematics. Five years of age separate each from the next. First there is I, Ottile; then Impie at Dongg's; then Zerpette, at the cottage, and Freitzke, in the kitchen. But we are not at all close. It is something in the blood. Our father is now a recluse and will tolerate only Zerpette, who of course hopes to gain his wealth when he dies."

"No doubt you remember Dr. Dacre."

Ottile uttered a coarse laugh. "How could I not remember him? He seduced my innocence! He swore that the love of Faurence and Ottile would become as renowned as the bonds between Prince Wortimer and the Silk Fairy, or if I preferred, that between Macellino Brunt and Cora Besong. Never had I heard a man speak in such rhapsodies! I told him, 'Take me! Introduce me to these famous ardors!' But his duties interfered. He and my father never made a good pair. Father was cautious; Faurence was daring. Father would apply a salve; Faurence would thrust the patient into one of his expensive machines and perform a remarkable operation. 'Soothe!' was my father's watchword. 'Cut!' cried

Faurence. They were together four years and then had a terrible quarrel. Faurence was sent packing, but my father kept all of Faurence's wonderful machines to pay for the money Faurence owed him. I heard the news and sorrowfully went to pack my clothes: I was at that time attached to my father and I did not want to leave Masmodo. I brought my luggage out to the street and stood waiting, dressed in my best. At last Impie came running to tell me that Faurence had left without me."

"What an awkward situation!"

"True. Faurence was really a cad."

"Where did he go next?"

"He went to try his luck on Skalkemond. Even I could have advised against this, for the Skalks above all are proper and orderly. Everything must be done just so, and this is not at all Faurence's way. Before two years had passed he caused a great scandal and was expelled from Skalkemond. So then, what should he do but return here, all pride and audacity! I reminded him of our holy love, but he would hear nothing of it; unfortunately I had gained a bit of weight. Faurence approached my father to buy back his machines, for half their value, and Father refused to listen; so what did Faurence do but open a new practice, and who should he select for his nurse and confidante? not me, but Impie! It seems as if she'd always had her eye on him, the drogbatte! Ah well, she's no better off now than I."

Hetzel saw that a comment would be in order. "Worse, I should say. At least you have retained your dignity!"

Ottile nodded with a vigor that set her blonde curls shaking. "Her surroundings are sordid; I, at least, deal with gentlemen."

Hetzel suggested that a taste or two of sublume brandy might sit well with the cider; Ottile endorsed the proposal.

Hetzel said thoughtfully: "I must say that conditions at Masmodo would hardly seem to justify the presence of two medical men."

"Correct! Although there is more business than might appear, what with Arsh and Dog-beards all along the coast, and the sublime orchardists up Joko Slope. About this time Father became ill and retired from practice and all the custom went to Faurence; for a time he and that unpleasant Impie were the busiest folk in Masmodo. Both day and night, no doubt. At any rate Faurence paid my father his money and recovered his wonderful equipment, and for good measure took over the dispensary as well. He wanted the cottage but Father refused to move. Zerpette was now taking care of him, and he was quite comfortable among his mementos; why inconvenience himself?"

"Why indeed?" Hetzel proffered the bottle. "A taste of this excellent brandy?"

"With pleasure."

Hetzel poured generously. "Please don't interrupt your account; you tell a most vivid tale."

"There is more to come. Faurence began to do remarkable work. One of the Arsh—what was his name? Sabin Cru—fell from his boat. A scrag went after him and plucked him like daisy. They hauled him out in a laundry basket; there wasn't enough left of Sabin to furnish a good grip. But Faurence went to work with a will. He did a grand job, and for certain kept the life inside Sabin Cru, and after that all the Arsh came to Dr. Dacre, and even the Dog-beards, although some were deterred by a rumor."

"What rumor?"

Ottile looked carefully right and left. "Who knows what the truth is? Does it sound credible that Dr. Dacre had a secret laboratory up the coast at Tinkum's Bar, where he conducted odd experiments and tried to cross a Dog-beard with a Flamboyard?"

"Offhand, no," said Hetzel. "However, I don't know what might be a Dog-beard, much less a Flamboyard."

"Dog-beards are no-hopers—beach folk; you find them mostly out at this end of the Torpeltines. You've never seen a Flamboyard?"

"Never."

"You've got a treat coming. They're our most important indigenes: feathered two-legged fruit eaters, the most gaudy and bizarre creatures imaginable. They have pink and purple plumes and orange fluff balls and golden horns. Why Faurence would want to tamper with such things is beyond imagination; any sensible person would know such a trick to be impossible. Still, someone—everybody thinks it was Father—turned in information. The Medical Inspector came down here posthaste and made no end of a row; if Faurence were innocent at Tinkum's Bar, he'd done something else as bad. He closed office and left Masmodo, and never came back."

"And when was this?"

"That would be about two years ago, more or less."

"Where did he go next?"

Ottile gave a voluminous shrug. "Impie might know. She dressed herself in her finery, packed her bags, took them out into the street and waited, but as before, Faurence never came by. After a bit she took her luggage back into the house and changed her clothes. Impie even now refuses to discuss Faurence Dacre, though once in a while I try to reminisce with her."

"Faurence Dacre seems a man of flexible principles."

"Impie and I are agreed on this, at least."

"Would your father know Faurence Dacre's present whereabouts?"

Ottile gave her head a pitying shake, for Hetzel's lack of perception. "Of all the folk of the Gaean Reach,

Father hates one man more than all others. That person is Faurence Dacre. But his pride prevents him from speaking Dacre's name, or even listening to the name spoken."

"What of Dacre's expensive equipment?"

"Still at the dispensary. Would you like to see it?"

"Very much! You are a remarkable storyteller and my curiosity is aroused."

"Among other things?" asked Ottile with a coy glance.

"But is it possible?" Hetzel inquired. "I refer, of course, to the dispensary."

"Of course it is possible," said Ottile, "since I have the key."

"Dr. Leuvil will not object?"

"What if he does? It is none of his affair."

CHAPTER 10

Companionably seizing Hetzel's arm, Ottile led the way up the slope. The sky blazed with stars; wind sighed through the sneezewoods. An irregular line of dim lights twisting and angling across the water charted the route to Dongg's Tavern, where a festoon of red and green lanterns promised to ease dry throats.

Dr. Leuvil's stark white cottage stood to one side of the road, the dispensary to the other. "Here we are," said Ottile. "Masmodo Dispensary, and not so bad a place, or so I'm told."

Ottile produced a cylinder which she touched to the code plate. The door swung open. She turned on lights. "This is the reception room: serviceable but not impressive. I myself painted the pictures on the wall."

"You have a sensitive touch."

"Thank you. This is the reception office, and yonder are the examination rooms. There was Dr. Dacre's private office. His papers and files have been removed of course, but otherwise—" Ottile made a vague gesture.

Hetzel went to examine the photographs which hung on the wall. "And who are these folk?"

Ottile walked along the wall, identifying such scenes as she was able. "—my father and the four girls, when we were quite young. Ah, look at me, how trusting and true! Was I not a dear child? . . . This is Dr. Dacre and the Arsh Sabin Cru. Notice the fearful damage which was done."

Hetzel saw the torso of a staring-eyed Arsh lying naked on a hospital bed. Behind stood Dr. Faurence
Dacre, smiling faintly, as if aware that the salvage he
had worked could only excite the viewer's awe. He
asked, "And what happened to Sabin Cru?"

"Hard to say. The Arsh won't tolerate deformities.
Like as not they drowned him. Impie of course would
know as to that. This is the nicest of the patients' rooms;
shall we just take a peep?"

"It hardly seems worth the trouble," said Hetzel. "I'm
more interested in technical matters."

"They've locked the door," said Ottile. She gave the
knob a fretful tug, then quickly turned and threw open
the door across the hall. "Examine this room; it is also
very nice."

"One hospital room is much like another," said
Hetzel. "Where are the operating chambers?"

"Through here." Ottile ushered him into a room
which occupied half of the entire structure. "What do
you think of this?"

Hetzel, who had been expecting one or two modest
pieces of special equipment, looked back and forth in
wonder. The chamber had been divided into bays, each
housing a specialized mechanism of obvious value. Ottile nodded wisely at Hetzel's marveling comments.
"Look at this thing here—I don't know its name, but it's
used during operations. The doctor stands nowhere near
the patient, but in this booth. This mask fits over his
head. By pushing his head forward he magnifies his field
of vision; by drawing back he reduces it. His hands and
arms fit into these gauntlets; the motions of his fingers
control miniaturized tools; with the foot pedals he
selects his equipment. With clear and magnified vision,
with perfectly controlled tools in his nerveless grip, the
doctor performs delicate operations with ease. If he
wants to work internally, he puts a pellet into the body
which he guides through stomach and intestines by magnetic beams. Meanwhile it transmits back a picture of

what it sees. At any particular spot the pellet can discharge medicine or heat, or work with small tools; then it is brought back out of the body."

"Marvelous," said Hetzel. "And this affair?"

"Something to do with eyes, so I have been told: a machine for cutting and indexing optic nerves between retina and brain, for eye transplants."

"Remarkable! And here?"

Ottile giggled. "It's a baby compressor, to help mothers in labor." She explained the functioning of the mechanism.

"Ingenious. And over here . . ."

Ottile said: "Oh, let's not talk about these ridiculous machines." She billowed forward and Hetzel was trapped between the wall and a gurney. "It's wonderful to meet a sympathetic man," murmured Ottile. "Sometimes I feel as if life is passing me by . . ."

A peremptory rap-rap-rap at the door. Hetzel darted away to safety. "Who's there?" called Ottile in a brassy voice.

"It's Zerpette. Is that you, Ottile? What are you up to this time of night?"

Ottile surged toward the door, but Hetzel outpaced her and flung it wide. "Come in, come in!"

Zerpette stood in the light, blinking crossly. "And what is your business here?"

"I am inspecting the dispensary. Is Dr. Leuvil still awake?"

Zerpette backed away from the door. Hetzel, looking past her, saw a gaunt shape on the verandah silhouetted against the light from within. He pushed past Zerpette, crossed the street, stood at the foot of the stairs. "Dr. Leuvil?"

"Young man, I have retired from practice. I give no interviews; I do not care for conversation." The voice was low, plangent, harsh.

"Nevertheless," said Hetzel, "you are a member of the human race, and presumably not irresponsible. I wish to locate Faurence Dacre, and in all civility you might supply me his address."

The gray face thrust even further forward; the milk-gray eyes peered at Hetzel. "Who are you? What do you want with Dr. Dacre?"

"I am Miro Hetzel. The name will mean nothing to you. I am an effectuator. Faurence Dacre has done my client harm. I wish to effect a remedy."

"Only this, and I will say no more. Dr. Dacre is a brilliant man. He made his mark here at Masmodo and then departed. He confided no hint of his plans to anyone; he left no address, nor have any of us received the slightest information as to his present whereabouts. This is all I can tell you."

Hetzel watched the stooped figure shuffle into the house. Zerpette slipped in after him. Hetzel turned slowly around to find himself alone. Ottile, sensing the elusiveness of Hetzel's manner, had departed.

Hetzel descended the main street, past the hotel to the waterfront. After a cautious appraisal of the area he walked out along the creaking docks to Dongg's Tavern, from which issued a grinding music of electric stringed instruments, punctuated by nasal howls of simulated emotion. Hetzel entered the tavern.

A dozen Arsh sat hunched over iron pots of beer. Behind the bar Impie stood languid and aloof.

Hetzel went to a corner of the bar and presently Impie condescended to glance in his direction.

"Yes sir?"—her voice as flat as yesterday's beer.

Hetzel said: "I'll have another of those rum punches, despite your sister's opinion of them."

Impie raised her invisible eyebrows. "Ottile? What does she know about it?"

"Nothing really. She had very odd ideas."

Impie looked away and sniffed. "An avalanche of sheer femininity. That's how someone once described her."

"She is overwhelming, for a fact. Who is 'Sabin Cru'?"

"One of the Arsh. What of him?"

"An Arsh? Ah, well."

Impie leaned across the counter, eyes sparkling. "What do you mean 'Ah, well'?"

"Nothing really. Dr. Dacre must have been an impressive fellow. If Sabin Cru had not died—"

"Who said Sabin had died?"

"He isn't dead? Does Dr. Dacre still look after him?"

"How would I know?" asked Impie crossly.

"I was given to understand that you were acquainted with both Dr. Dacre and Sabin Cru."

"I am not acquainted with any Arsh."

"Naturally not. How does Sabin Cru support himself now?"

"You'd have to ask his mother."

"Ottile said he was with Dr. Dacre."

"Hah!" Impie's laugh was rich with scorn. "What would she know?"

"The mother doesn't live with you then?"

Impie's face worked in a peculiar fashion as the emotions of wonder, fury, and incredulity warred with each other. She glared speechlessly at Hetzel, and finally said: "Are you a lunatic? What is wrong with you to say such a stupid thing?"

"Sorry," said Hetzel in a subdued voice. "I misunderstood. To tell the truth I wasn't really listening to the—"

Impie's face was now congested. "Sabin Cru's mother is named Farucas. She lives ten miles down the coast. Go there yourself! You will see!"

"I'm sure it was a mistake. Where can I find Dr. Dacre? I'll straighten it all out once and for all."

"You and your Dr. Dacre!" screamed Impie, breaking a bottle on the counter. "You and he can—"

Hetzel rose to his feet and departed Dongg's Tavern. Impie's tirade gradually diminished as he returned across the swaying piers to the shore.

CHAPTER 11

In the morning Freitzke served Hetzel his breakfast. Hetzel decided that in all likelihood she knew nothing of Faurence Dacre; after all. Zerpette's turn was next. He crossed the tree-shaded main street to the post office and sent a telegram to Conwit Clent at Dandyl Villa, Junis, Cassander, Thesse:

I have discovered a confused situation but may know more within the next few days. The outcome, from your point of view, is still uncertain. I will keep you informed.

Hetzel descended the main street to the waterfront and walked out upon the pier, where he stopped to consider a fishing boat with red, white and black Arsh symbols painted around the gunwales.

An Arsh in a loose white shirt and black trousers crouched in the cockpit, fitting a new section of coaming.

"Is this boat for hire?" asked Hetzel.

The Arsh rose to his feet and wiping his hands on his breeches, surveyed Hetzel with care. "Well then, Merner*, where do you want to go?"

"Ten or fifteen miles along the coast, perhaps as far as

*Merner: usual polite appellative of the Jingkens' worlds.

Tinkum's Bar. Does it matter?"

"Not particularly. Jump aboard then, Merner, let's get underway."

"Not so fast. We have not yet settled upon a price."

Negotiations required several minutes, but at last Hetzel jumped down into the boat.

The converter sighed; electrified water surged back from drive strips; the boat angled among the piers, rounded the breakwater, and slid out upon the slow swells of the Mondial Ocean. "Now where, Merner?" asked the Arsh.

"I am a journalist," Hetzel explained. "I have been assigned to write an article upon Dr. Dacre and his work. Are you acquainted with him?"

"Not at all."

"What of Sabin Cru—do you know him?"

"He should have been drowned. It is bad luck to nurture half a corpse: you may so inform your readers."

"I will make a note," said Hetzel. "I am informed that Sabin Cru now lives with his mother Farucas."

"I was there when Impie informed you," said the boatman. "She told you of a great deal more."

"She has a gift for expression," said Hetzel. "So then, take me to the house of Farucas."

"As you like."

Alongside white beaches drove the boat, past slanting coconut palms, purple and mauve gangee, pink jorgiana, lianas trailing a hundred feet of white trumpet blossoms. The boat slid across turquoise tinted shallows and dark blue depths; looking over the side Hetzel saw all manner of sea life: white gloves with black ribbons; needles of blue fire darting and stopping; a snow-white fish ten feet long with a wedge-shaped knob of a head four feet across; a creature which the boatman named a sea scrag, somewhat like a fifteen-foot scorpion, with pincers at each end; uncountable small fish.

The boatman pointed. "Tinkum's Bar; Farucas' house."

The house stood on a graded flat among fruit trees and a line of coco palms: a structure of crystallized sand, far more substantial than Hetzel had expected. From the verandah an Arsh woman watched the boat. Hetzel asked, "Is that Farucas?"

"There she stands."

"Let's go in."

The boatman made fast to a concrete pier; Hetzel jumped ashore. He climbed a path to the house. The woman apparently had not stirred from where he had seen her first. "Hello," called Hetzel. "Are you Farucas?"

"Yes, I am Faurcas."

Hetzel joined her upon the verandah; the woman looked at him with apprehension. Like all Arsh she was squat, with heavy shoulders and short heavy legs. Her ears, already pendulous, were expanded even farther with plugs of carved vermillion; her nose hung heavy and crooked, like a faulty cucumber. "Sir, what do you want here?"

"Where is Sabin Cru?"

"He is not here," said Farucas with prim finality.

From inside the house came a scraping sound, as of a chair being pulled across the floor. Hetzel said: "He is not here, you say. Then who makes that noise?"

Before Farucas could respond Hetzel had stepped past her and into the house.

He found himself in a long room with white plastered walls, divided into two sections by a low counter, the far end of which supported trays of mush and cooked fruit. Behind the counter stood three splendid beings a foot taller than Hetzel. Each showed a pointed parchment-white visage surmounted first by a pair of twisted gilded horns, then a crest of scarlet, gray, and orange plumes. Under the head a collar of black hair hung over the heavy thorax, while the occipital crest continued down the back. A colorful and picturesque group, thought Hetzel; the creatures would seem to merit their popular appellation: Flamboyards. They treated Hetzel to stares of haughty inquiry, then continued with their feeding. A fourth Flamboyard entered the room on the human side of the counter, to stand stock still watching Hetzel: a creature not so tall as the others, heavier and apparently more solid, with a large near-globular head.

Farucas cried out, "As I told you: these are not Sabin Cru!"

"So I see. Who paid for this expensive house?"

Farucas made a gesture. "Oh, I pay money."

"And where did the money come from?"

"Yes; it is money."

"Sabin Cru gives you money?"

"Yes, that is true," said Farucas. "He is good to me."

"And where does Sabin Cru get money?"

"I don't know. Maybe Doctor."

"Where is Dr. Dacre?"

"I don't know about Doctor."

"I want to tell him about tax, but now I talk to you."

"I don't know about tax."

"No, because this is not your house! Dr. Dacre doesn't want any old thing living here. You get out."

"No, no! Doctor wants me to feed the Flams!"

"Oh! You take care of the Flams?"

"Yes, that is true!"

"Then you must pay the tax."

"No tax on those things," declared Farucas without conviction.

"That's where you're wrong. A very big tax is due. I am empowered to take the money."

Farucas looked uneasily over her shoulder. "I don't have money."

"Then I must collect from Doctor or from Sabin Cru. Tell me where, or I must file a derogatory report!"

Farucas again looked over her shoulder, as if seeking help from the Flamboyards. The three tall individuals ate without interest; the fourth had departed the room.

Farucas said hopelessly, "I don't know where is Doctor Dacre. Sabin is in Masmodo. He stays with old Leuvil."

"Old Leuvil, eh? I talk to old Leuvil; he does not say Sabin is there."

"Leuvil keep Sabin because of Doctor Dacre. They work together a long time; they are such friends."

"Yes, that is possible." Hetzel moved to examine a photograph on the wall. "Who is this? Could it be Sabin Cru?"

Farucas nodded pridefully. "That is now Sabin. He is happy that he is alive and well."

Hetzel returned to the boat. The Arsh boatman cast off and turned back toward Masmodo. After a few minutes he asked in a sly voice: "Did you find Sabin Cru?"

"No. He is in Masmodo, according to his mother."

"I could have told you that."

"No doubt you could have," said Hetzel. "Why did Impie tell me he was with his mother?"

"She told you to ask his mother."

"Perhaps; I don't remember all that accurately. What else do you know that you haven't told me?"

"I know why Dr. Leuvil called in the Medical Inspector on Dr. Dacre."

"And why was that?"

"Is the information worth ten SVU?"

"Probably not."

"How much is it worth then?"

"Very hard to say."

"Ah, well, you'll hear it free of charge from someone else. Farucas keeps three Flamboyards; did you see them?"

"Yes," said Hetzel. "I did."

"A rumor started that Dr. Dacre had used antirejection serum to construct Flamboyard hybrids, and

Farucas was declared to be the mother. So went the story."

"And quite a story it is, if true."

"Merner Stipes, the Medical Inspector, made things hot for Dr. Dacre, so maybe something was going on."

"So why does Dr. Leuvil now keep Sabin Cru?"

The boatman shrugged. "Leuvil has also locked away Dr. Dacre's machines. Sabin alone profits from the discord. If he were here I would drown him at once. The sea has claimed him, and will never let him go."

"The question then remains: where is Dr. Dacre?"

"He comes and goes. He might return tomorrow."

"Possibly so. What else do you know?"

"Nothing, Merner, that you would wish to pay for."

From the Masmodo dock Hetzel went directly to the post office where he communicated with the Azimuth Effectuation Group at Narghuys. After an exchange of polite pleasantries with the director, Hetzel requested the services of five top-quality operatives. These arrived at Masmodo on the following day and Hetzel explained his requirements: "Notice the house and dispensary on the hill yonder. In one or the other resides a most important witness in a case, who must not be allowed to slip through our fingers. Both house and dispensary must be watched constantly: two men by day, three men by night. Work out the schedule to suit yourselves. Plan for every contingency. If you need more help, call Azimuth: I prefer too many men to too few. Be discreet, but do not attempt to be invisible. The woman may come and go, but be sure it is the woman; do not be deceived by padding and a wig, or any other subterfuge. Is everything clear?"

Questions were asked; Hetzel clarified all areas of ambiguity, then departed Masmodo.

CHAPTER 12

Conwit Clent received a telegram at Dandyl Villa. It read:

The situation has reached a critical stage. Your presence is needed. Please come on the instant to Narghuys, Gietersmond. Meet me at the Cosmolux Hotel, Suite 100.
I will expect you by earliest scheduled transport.

Arriving at the Cosmolux Hotel, Clent was received by Hetzel in the foyer of Suite 100. "You are the last to arrive, but still in good time. Our business now proceeds."

Clent stopped short. "What is going on? Please explain to me."

"I would do so with pleasure, Xtl Clent, except that the others are becoming restless, and we still have much to do. Come this way; I will introduce you."

Hetzel ushered Clent into the sitting room. Those already present fell silent and scrutinized Clent with an interest more direct and intent than might have suited ordinary circumstances.

"At last," said Hetzel, "our group is complete, except for a person whom we will shortly join. Gentlemen, this is Xtl Conwit Clent, of Thesse. Around the room are Lazar, Baron Keurboom from Disten; Dr. Aartemus of the Academy of Medical Sciences at Narghuys; Merner Ander Stipes, Medical Inspector for the Torpeltines; Dominie Dandrue Cheasling, Headmaster at the Trembling Waters Academy, also on Thesse; the Honorable Shaide Casbain of Meurice, Skalkemond. Among us we represent many eras in the life of Faurence Dacre. Not all, of course. A certain Dr. Leuvil must still be consulted, and then—"

Baron Keurboom made a convulsive clutching gesture. "Are these preliminaries necessary? Let us get to the point! Where is Faurence?"

"Quite right, Baron," said Hetzel. "We should delay no longer. A vehicle awaits us; we will—"

"Must we travel further then?"

"I consider it essential, Baron. At Masmodo we bridge the final gap in the life of Faurence Dacre. The man who typifies that period is something of a recluse, but no matter; the situation must somehow resolve itself. If everyone is ready? Good. Follow me, if you will . . ."

CHAPTER 13

The aircraft flew along the chain of the Torpeltines, slanted down upon Jamus Amaha, and landed at Masmodo, behind the post office. As the group alighted a stocky gray-haired man approached and took Hetzel aside. The two spoke together several minutes, then Hetzel turned to the others. "Everything appears to be in order. This is my associate, Bruno Imhalter, of the Azimuth Effectutation Group. A word or two about Dr. Leuvil. At one time he was Faurence Dacre's partner, then his competitor, and finally his enemy. Yonder is his cottage, and across the way a dispensary, which contains a considerable amount of Dr. Dacre's equipment. In the dispensary resides a man who is both familiar with Dr. Dacre and who must know his whereabouts: a certain Sabin Cru. I and Merner Imhalter have gone to great pains to ensure that he has not been removed from the vicinity."

"All very well," grumbled Clent, "but where is Dacre?"

"Faurence Dacre is unpredictable," said Hetzel. "We may find that he has resorted to a bizarre disguise. As we all know, Faurence Dacre enjoys the sensation of extrahuman power, to which the anonymity of a disguise sometimes contributes. But now we call upon Dr.

Leuvil, although I cannot guarantee a cordial welcome."

Their approach to the cottage did not go unnoticed. As the group climbed the steps up to Dr. Leuvil's verandah, the door swung open and Zerpette Leuvil looked forth, round face glowing with rage, her ridiculous blond ringlets bouncing and jerking. "Please! We do not want to see you. Go away, you have no business here! Or I will call the constable!"

"To no purpose, Miss Leuvil; he would only assure you that we are respectable persons, with legitimate purposes for our visit. If you will announce us, we will transact our business as quickly as possible."

Zerpette drew a deep breath, charging her lungs for an extended defiance, but from within sounded a few words in a terse voice. Zerpette flounced back and flung open the door. "In then, all of you! Wipe your feet on the mat. You are not here by my wishes."

The group filed portentously into the side sitting room. "Dr. Leuvil?" spoke Hetzel politely. "I believe that we have already met, if informally."

The unwilling host, hunched behind a desk, responded only with a grunt; then, noting Imhalter, he declared angrily: "You have put a surveillance upon this house! What is your purpose?"

Hetzel responded: "The affair is simple. We have been told that Sabin Cru is under your care."

"What of that?"

"Why have you taken charge of Sabin Cru?"

"It is none of your affair."

"I am not so sure. Is Sabin Cru not Dr. Dacre's concern?"

"Dr. Dacre has made commitments not yet fulfilled: to myself and to others of my family."

"In that case," asked Hetzel, "why should we not join forces?"

"I have learned to trust no living man. Everything I

have worked for has been blasted, through trust. No more. I am not interested in your problems; you must do your own work; and now I ask you to go. Do not harass me, a tired sick man who can barely see."

"You have all our sympathy," said Hetzel. "Permit us a word with Sabin Cru and we will allow you to rest."

"I will permit nothing."

"Then we must act without your permission."

"That is at your discretion. I cannot force decency upon you."

"Be so good as to summon him."

"No. Leave the house. He is not here."

Zerpette bustled forward. "How long must you stay?"

"Not much longer. Merner Imhalter, look into the dispensary, if you please. Did you speak, Dr. Leuvil?"

"Go. Leave the house."

Hetzel followed Imhalter out upon the verandah, and gave orders which brought a grim smile to Imhalter's face.

Hetzel returned into the sitting room. "Merner Imhalter and his men are bringing Sabin Cru here. If you prefer, Dr. Leuvil, we will ask our questions on the verandah."

"I prefer to hear whatever you have to say."

"As you wish." Hetzel spoke to his group. "You may wonder why both Dr. Leuvil and I set such store by Sabin Cru. He is an ordinary Arsh, notable only for the terrible mauling he took from a sea scrag. But he represents for Dr. Dacre a masterpiece, so to speak; the restoration of life to a few shreds of moribund tissue. Even Dr. Leuvil will agree that the work was well done. Correct, Doctor?"

"Dr. Dacre beyond doubt is supreme in his field."

Several minutes passed. Conwit Clent started to speak, then curbed himself; twice Lazar, Baron Keurboom made his now-familiar clutching clenching gesture.

A tap at the door; Imhalter and one of his operators entered, in company with a man in a soiled white hospital gown.

Hetzel signaled the newcomer to a seat. "We have put you to some inconvenience, which I fear must increase. He looked toward Zerpette. "You are a doctor's daughter, and in any event must be aware of the human body." Hetzel turned to his friends. "Without attempting to extract every dramatic nuance from this situation, I will merely present to you Sabin Cru, the one-time Arsh fisherman, and now as you see."

AnderStipes, the District Medical Inspector, leaned forward in sudden interest. "He's no Arsh. Unless he's a half-breed—but he doesn't even look like a half-breed."

"He's not exactly pure Arsh," said Hetzel. "Imhalter, if you will, remove Sabin Cru's gown."

Sabin Cru resisted only briefly. The gown was removed; Sabin Cru sat naked except for underwear.

"I will ask you all to inspect Sabin Cru closely," said Hetzel. "Certain of his adjuncts may well be familiar to you."

"Unless I am much mistaken," said Dr. Aartemus, "those are my two legs. And my feet."

"So that is the way the wind blows," cried Shaide Casbain in sudden excitement. "There is my left arm; notice the tattoo."

"The right arm is mine," declared Dominie Cheasling. "I have long worn this plaz and steel contraption without complaint, but no longer."

Stipes the Medical Inspector nodded grimly. "Dr. Dacre once told me to keep my nose out of his affairs or I might need a new nose. He meant every word."

"Faurence told me I used my jaw too much," Baron Keurboom remarked dolefully. "The result has been the same."

Conwit Clent said, "I cannot instantly identify my

own property, but I am hopeful. Miro Hetzel, your reputation has not been overstated. How did you learn all this?"

"It is a complex process of integrating facts, then adding a lucky guess or two," said Hetzel, always reluctant to make his work seem too simple. But now, looking around the room, he saw that more was expected of him. "Of course there were interesting incidents along the way. A few days ago I visited Sabin Cru's mother at Tinkum's Bar. While there I noticed a photograph of Sabin Cru as he is now, and my suspicions were verified. Thenceforth my first anxiety was to guard him from accident, escape, murder, or any other violent incident. I now deliver this property into your hands."

"All very well," said Shaide Casbain, "but what do we do with it?"

Hetzel shrugged. "Across the way is a miniature hospital; we have eminent medical men in our group: Dr. Aartemus, Dr. Leuvil—"

"I am retired; I cannot see to work."

"That leads us to a new speculation. Just when, Dr. Leuvil, did your eyes start going bad?"

"Not long ago. Three years. Then as if overnight."

"You know that in the dispensary is equipment to expedite ocular transplant?"

"Yes, of course. Your implications are ridiculous. Dr. Dacre would never dare."

"What color were your eyes originally?"

"Blue. They have changed with my disability."

Hetzel nodded. "Let us review your association with Dr. Dacre. He came out as your associate. Ottile was then your nurse—"

"Yes; she would not leave him alone, the rumplinga. I threw him out and threw her out, and Impie became my nurse."

"Exactly. Dr. Dacre went to Skalkemond. In due

course he ran afoul of Merner Casbain and the stringent Skalkemond law as well, and hastily returned to Masmodo. Here he set up a rival practice, hired—or induced—Impie away from her father.

"During this period he salvaged Sabin Cru, but I doubt if his great idea had yet occurred to him, for he had now begun his Flamboyard experiments. Dr. Leuvil reported them to Merner Stipes, who came to Masmodo and rescinded Dr. Dacre's license. Once again Dr. Dacre was forced to leave. Impie, no longer welcome at home, took a job in the tavern. Dr. Dacre went to Cassander, and became successful, but all the time he reflected upon his various enemies, from Dominie Cheasling, who had expelled him from Trembling Waters, to Ander Stipes, and finally poor Conwit Clent. Dr. Dacre traveled frequently, and each time he traveled Sabin Cru received new equipment. Eyes? Not Dr. Leuvil's eyes, which were blue.

"Dr. Dacre found himself spending considerable time here at Masmodo. How was he able to conceal his presence? I can describe one possible way. Dr. Leuvil died one night, as if in his sleep. The next morning Dr. Dacre appeared and was able to console Zerpette, now a lass both rollicking and buxom. Faurence Dacre quietly disposed of the body, practiced walking hunched over with a cane, and Dr. Leuvil was more of a recluse than ever. Imhalter, if you please."

Imhalter, seizing the gray curls, pulled away wig and filmy mask of gray wrinkles, to reveal the features of Faurence Dacre.

"The disguise was indeed bizarre," said Hetzel critically. "Ottile however mentioned that all the family was left-handed. On the first occasion I met Dr. Leuvil, I noticed that he was right-handed. Therefore, 'Dr. Leuvil' was not Dr. Leuvil. Who could he be? Who else but Dr. Dacre?

"Freitzke of course had been sent to assist Ottile; after all, it was now Zerpette's turn. All the while in Cassander Faurence assiduously courted Perdhra Olruff, only to lose her to a better man. Imhalter, I hope you have taken his weapons?"

"All we can find, Xtl Hetzel: a Vaast ray and a pair of squibboons."

"So now, I have discharged my task. You gentlemen must decide what next to do. I have suggested the hospital yonder; why should not Dr. Aartemus communicate with an appropriate number of expert surgeons who are willing to perform certain unofficial operations: I might also suggest that if any deficiencies occur—for instance, Sabin Cru is blameless; why should he suffer a new tragedy? Better that the organs he must now give up be replaced by the gentleman who initiated the process."

"I agree in all respects," said Conwit Clent. "Dr. Aartemus, what is your feeling in the matter?"

"I am somewhat constrained by the presence of Merner Stipes, the Torpeltines District Medical Inspector."

"Feel no constraint on my part!" declared Ander Stipes. "In fact, I resign my post as of this instant. When the operations are finished I will reconsider; but as of now, regard me as a collaborator."

"Then there seems no further reason for delay," said Dr. Aartemus. "Except—er, what of Zerpette?"

Zerpette said in a dry voice: "I have learned much which I did not know, including the existence of Perdhra Olruff at Cassander. You may ignore me as well. I am finished. It is now Freitzke's turn."

CHAPTER 14

At Dandyl Villa, Hetzel rendered Conwit Clent an accounting of his expenses. "They run somewhat high, but men like Bruno Imhalter do not come cheap, and as you know I have traveled considerably."

"Not another word!" declared Clent. "I am intensely pleased; furthermore each member of the group has insited upon sharing the expense, so little enough is coming from my own pocket."

"In that case," said Hetzel, "the problem no longer exists. Allow me to wish you and your wife the happiest of marriages, with both loyal sons and dutiful daughters."

"I hope the same, Miro Hetzel. But what of Faurence Dacre?"

"He is now under the care of Freitzke and Sabin Cru."

"Will he not eventually work further mischief?"

"The chances would seem scant. Sabin Cru, remember, would be the first to suffer if Dacre ever again required the return of his members. Remember also that the Arsh are a superstitious race; they believe that an incomplete man brings bad luck. We have probably heard the last of Faurence Dacre. Still, the next time I pass Gietersmond, I will visit Masmodo and make a casual enquiry. It is always interesting to look over the scene of a previous case."

* THE END *

JACK VANCE

Born in 1920, Jack Vance served in the US Merchant Navy during WWII, and has supported himself at times by a variety of jobs ranging from construction worker to jazz musician. Now one of the most widely read and well-respected authors of our time, he has written more than forty novels and seventy-five shorter works in the fields of fantasy, mystery, horror and science fiction. Two of his novels were adopted for television, where he was one of the primary writers for the "Captain Video" series. Some of his richly deserved awards include the rare Triple Crown of speculative fiction: the Hugo (for *The Dragon Masters*, 1963,) the Nebula (for *The Last Castle*, 1966, which also won a Hugo,) and the Edgar (for *The Man in the Cage*, 1960, from the Mystery Writers of America).

He is known especially for his crafty wit, brilliant use of color and his ability to depict both virtue and poltroonery across the entire spectrum of human interaction. His hobbies include blue-water sailing, house remodeling and the four-string banjo. He lives in the hills above Oakland, California with his son John and his wife Norma.